HANDBOOK ON TROUGHS

Chapters

Reprinted from the *Bulletin of the American Rock Garden Society*
Guest Editor, Joyce Fingerut
Editor, Gwen Kelaidis

Troughs:

A Special Love Affair

by Gwen Kelaidis

I am that variety of gardener who gardened although I lived in rented apartments, tilling first one yard, then another. In 1975 I inherited two troughs from my friend Jim Sawyer and planted them to sempervivums and sedums. They sat on either side of the sidewalk leading to the front door, taking the humble place of sentinel lions and eliciting many questions from passers-by. And when I moved to Colorado, they moved with me.

So began my adventures with troughs, but it wasn't until 1985 that I became a real devotee. Our friend Stan Metsker suggested pointedly that I plant anything important to me in troughs until we found a way to buy a house. It made sense, yet I had a large appetite for plants and would need many troughs.

I had tried my hand at making troughs in molds, and it was the unmolding process that was the problem. I have trouble even removing jello from its container. I tried the free-form trough, building upside-down in wet sand. Lumpy bowls with thick rims resulted, their shaved off bottoms usually not in quite the proper plane to have them sit flat when

turned right side up. Thankfully, Stan offered to construct troughs for me, provided only that I would plant them for display at the 1986 Interim International Rock Garden Plant Conference in Boulder, Colorado. So began an extra-garden affair that has continued to this day.

A trough is a garden unto itself, a landscape and plant community complete on its own. The container frames and gives this landscape shape. Rocks and soil can be selected to suit the needs of the plants and can easily differ from those of the larger garden. The trough can be designed to represent a little slice of a natural ecosystem, or it may simply be a container with plants of similar stature and ecological needs, such as cactuses, or kabschia saxifrages. If I really want to grow a plant and can't meet the soil requirements in the garden, I dedicate a trough to it, as I've done with *Gentiana verna* (needing peaty soil) and *Petrophytum caespitosum* (requiring a tight, dry crevice).

There are three compelling reasons to place a plant in a trough rather than in the open garden.

Plants Don't Get Lost

Some plants are so small that they get lost in a rock garden. Examples include the tiny dryland *Penstemon pumilus*, choice *Talinum* species, such as *T. sedoides* (*T. okanoganense*), *T. brevifolium*, and *T. pulchellum*. *Lesquerella alpina* and *Penstemon acaulis* are almost that small, growing to an inch or two in diameter in some years. Other very slow growers include *Lepidium nanum* and *Kelseya uniflora*. In the garden such plants are easily overgrown by larger neighbors. They also have little visual impact even in bloom, unless planted in groups of five or more. Wouldn't we be lucky to have a dozen or two with which to experiment! In the meantime, I place them in troughs, where they are proportionately important and where I can keep an eye on them.

Plants Live Longer, Bloom Better

In the last eight years of growing dryland plants of western North America I have found that many simply survive *only* in troughs and not in the garden. Penstemons like *P. acaulis*, *P. laricifolius*, *P. angustifolius*, *P. humilis*, *P. caryi* are still blooming every year in troughs, while their seedpot mates have long ago died in the garden. *Astragalus spatulatus* and species of *Townsendia*, such as *T. hookeri* and *T. alpigena*, have long lives in these elevated homes. The ball cactuses, of which I am increasingly fond (*Echinocereus, Coryphantha, Mammilaria, Pediocactus, Sclerocactus*) seem to winter very well in troughs. Cactuses, especially opuntias, can change the design feel of a garden, but in a trough they can have a world of their own. Cactuses often self-sow, and seem happy with companions such as those mentioned earlier in this paragraph.

I can only speculate that this longer life for plants of the West has to do with the drier environment of the trough. All of my garden soils contain a large component of clay loam. In this climate with 12" to 15" of rain, some clay is advantageous, giving the soil the ability to hold some moisture longer. However, in wet spells when we receive afternoon thundershowers everyday for a week or two, plants in the garden may get too wet. In winter, also, in the cold north shade of evergreen trees—where there is no shade in summer because of the higher angle of the sun—even acantholimons seem to suffer. In the troughs it just seems that the soil stays drier.

Freedom of Design

That great old adage of rock gardening, "Use only one kind of rock," can be sidestepped by the simple use of troughs. My 1986 Conference troughs were a discovery ground for me, a wonderful field of experimentation. I used many different rock types, from rounded sandstone boulders, to gnarled limestone, to slate, to the pebbles of desert pavement, each in a different trough. I had the opportunity to build with all these different rocks on a scale without back strain, front-end loaders, or a large budget. In far-flung places of the West I picked up rocks that I thought would look attractive in a trough, along with smaller rocks and a variety of pebble sizes for mulch. The plastic bags of pebbles have been hard to keep track of in the potting shed (once a garage). I have developed a system of sorts, keeping extra rocks and pebbles for each trough in a gallon-size or larger pot, and the matching gravel inside in a plastic bag. Eventually the mulch needs to be topped up, what with watering, replanting and, in my case, toddlers. It helps to hold your hand over the mulch while watering, so that no gravel washes off. When there is simply no longer enough mulch, you are forced to return to the original location for more gravel—usually a great pleasure.

A favorite theme for design in a trough is to recreate a natural plant association. I try to achieve something of the feel of the landscape, using the primary or dominant plant types from the area. My Pikes Peak trough, then, had to include the famous *Telesonix jamesii*, the bright blue bells of *Mertensia alpina*, and still it is not really complete without *Eritrichium nanum, Primula angustifolia*, and *Androsace chamaejasme*. I have a trough from central Wyoming with dwarf sagebrush (*Artemisia arbuscula*), *Castilleja*, and a dainty *Erigeron*. I should add an *Astragalus* or two and the small creamy beauty *Physaria eburniflora*. The Laramie Plains trough has a glorious specimen of *Astragalus spatulatus*, along with *Townsendia exscapa*, a penstemon or two, *Selaginella densa* making a low, olive green patch of turf, and *Eriogonum flavum*. This trough I consider a great success, as plants are now self-sowing. I should mention that it is wonderful to have several plants of each species in the trough, echoing each other whether in bloom or out and giving the trough a sort of unity that a group of solitary beauties cannot achieve. Because of my interest in producing seeds, I prefer at least five plants of a kind in each trough.

Soil

My soils mixes vary. Each trough has different components, but all have some sand and most have gravel. Despite the recent bad reputation of these soil components, I find that sand and gravel improve the way water moves through the soil mix, making it easier to wet and faster to drain. Soil scientists speak of oxygen and air space, and sand and gravel often come out on the short end of the equations. This isn't surprising, since they are fairly large solid particles, and inside them there is no room for air and water. If a rock half as big as a pot is added to the soil of a container and the formula recalculated, the air space will be considerably reduced, but the plant roots, since they don't grow inside the rock, will not experience a decrease in available air. What has really changed for the plant is the inside *shape* of the pot. Similarly, large gravel in a mix doesn't impact the *air space* available to roots as much as the formulas imply but rather creates a convoluted soil *shape* within the container. Also, water moves more quickly through the pot along rock or gravel surfaces than it would through, say, a clay. The current formula neglects the factor of time. How *long* it takes for the air spaces to be cleared of water matters.

My peat trough has mostly peat and a little sand; the alpine troughs have some sand, some gravel, some clay loam, a little peat, and perhaps a little Turface; the dryland troughs have less gravel, usually no peat, perhaps more Turface. Turface is a baked clay product a bit like kitty litter, but baked harder, so that it doesn't break down. It makes the soil fluffier, and the only problem I have with it is that soil mixes with a high percentage of Turface tend to heave in winter. Sometimes I put more clay or more Turface in the bottom layer of soil in a trough, hoping that they will hold a little more water without being too oxygen-depleted. The upper soil layer of the trough is not so much different than the lower that the roots will be stopped at the interface—which is always irregular anyway. I abhor perlite in trough soils, because it floats to the top during watering. I will sometimes use spent potting soil containing perlite, but again, I bury it in the bottom layer of the soil.

Mountain Building

Only in a few cases, such as my desert pavement troughs, do I have the surface of the soil below the rim of the container. Generally I use three to five larger rocks to build a ridge, monolith, or outcrop. These add the dimension of height, the mystery of what's behind the rock, more niches for planting, and soil.

Watering

In Colorado it is necessary to water troughs every day in June, July, and August, unless one of those scattered thundershowers scatters your way. I prefer to water with a slow-running hose, the stream about twice the diameter of a pencil, often letting the rocks take the force of the water. I let the trough surface become completely covered with water to the brim of the container. It is my intention that every spot on the surface be covered with about 1/4" of water, and then I consider that the soil below is going to get enough moisture.

About half of my troughs have been located for three years now where they receive daily overhead water from my sprinkler system, designed to water small flats of seedlings. This works very well for the silver saxifrages, peat trough, and the true alpines, such as *Gentiana verna* and the Pikes Peak trough. Dryland plants from Wyoming grow well, but the mulch becomes covered with mosses. This disturbs me, but delights most Coloradoans who prize lush moss. Seedlings do come up in the moss—it just *looks* wrong to me.

Because of low humidity, intense sun, and wind, evaporation rates are very high here. I no longer attempt to grow plants in troughs containing less than a half-bushel of soil. They dry out too fast. I prefer containers that take about two bushels of soil mix.

Hot/Cold Protection

Temperatures sometimes fall as low as-25°F in Denver but within a day or two will again reach above 0°F. I don't protect my 35 or so troughs in any way from cold, not even by setting them on the ground, where temperatures probably change more slowly. I haven't noticed any winter losses. In summer, the small volume of soil is subject to heating to temperatures that may well be problematic for roots. I move all but the cactus well away from the east wall of the brick house, where the sun is a factor until almost 1 p.m. If it's really hot, I spray the outside of the troughs with water or spray the flagstone and hope that evaporative cooling will decrease the temperature below critical frizz.

Fertilizing

I think the most important fertilizing is to be done when the plants are in active growth, especially before flowering and, for roots, often in cool periods of early spring and early fall. I use Osmocote on the borders in late May and throw it at the troughs then too. It is only actively released in warm weather, so for bulbs and early spring bloomers like *Aquilegia jonesii*, I would think that a liquid application would be better. Perhaps a low-nitrogen, higher-phosphate blend like Peter's Blossom Booster would be most appropriate to rock garden plants staying in character and blooming their heads off. Three applications a year would be good; one is, of course, better than nothing.

Display

Troughs look great at entry ways, on steps, low walls, terraces, or even set into the garden proper. Do try putting some up on blocks or pedestals made with left-over hypertufa.

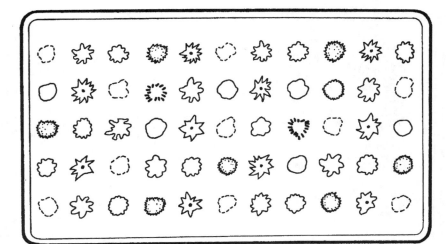

Charlesworth Trough
Year 1

SIZE: Length 30"   Width 20"   Height 8"

EXPOSURE: Morning sun

SOIL MIX: Coarse sand, Jiffy Mix, Osmocote, gravel; No SOIL

TOP DRESSING: Gravel or sand

—Allow about 12 square inches per plant

—Don't plant different species of the same genus in adjacent positions. This avoids confusion of names when labels break.

—Don't waste space with rocks, gnomes, etc.

—Plant as many Type 2 plants as you have or can afford.

—All the rest are Type 1a or 1c, but you can fill up with Type 3 and Type 5 if you haven't enough.

Gwen Kelaidis learned to garden at her mother's knee, pinching back tomatoes, weeding tall bearded irises, growing rose bushes, and eating raspberries. She later studied botanical taxonomy. Rock gardening was the inevitable end for such a combination. She now gardens in Denver, Colorado, with her two children, Eleni and Jesse, and husband Panayoti.

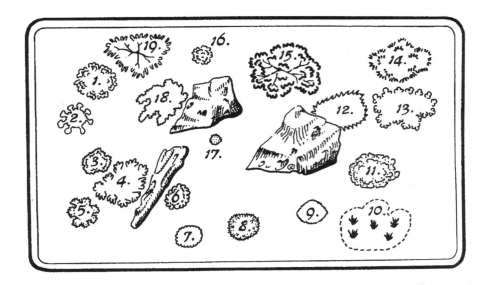

Charlesworth Trough
Years 2-3

SIZE: Length 30"   Width 20"   Height 8"

EXPOSURE: Morning sun

SOIL MIX: Coarse sand, Jiffy Mix, Osmocote, gravel; No Soil

TOP DRESSING: Gravel or sand

—All the Type 2 plants are now dead.
—Introduce *Chamaecyparis*, *Daphne*, pieces of tufa, and seedlings of *Lewisia rediviva* to fill in the gaps.

1. *Arabis bryoides*
2. *Eriogonum ovalifolium*
3. *Androsace carnea*
4. *Campanula raineri*
5. *Androsace mathildae*
6. *Campanula cochlearifolia*
7. *Draba rosularis*
8. *Saxifraga paniculata* 'Minutifolia'
9. *Draba rigida*
10. *Lewisia rediviva* seedlings

11. *Phlox pulvinata*
12. *Silene acaulis*
13. *Dicentra peregrina*
14. *Vitaliana primuliflora*
15. *Chamaecyparis* 'Snow'
16. *Draba bryoides*
17. *Eritrichium howardii*
18. *Androsace villosa*
19. *Daphne retusa*

Plants for Troughs

by Geoffrey Charlesworth

I should explain at the outset my attitude towards troughs, so that you will be under no illusion about expecting advice from me about actually planting troughs. I admire a well planted trough—"planted for effect"—which is stereotypically a cross between a Japanese landscape, a toy alp, and a doll house backyard, engagingly displaying two or three small lumps of tufa, a couple of dwarf conifers, and closely packed baby plants around the rocks. I admire it, but I don't want to do it myself. Beyond this innocent charm, troughs have at least two good reasons for existence as horticultural tools. The first is aesthetic: you can examine plants with greater ease and pleasure if they are in a trough at a comfortable height—between shin and elbow level. And some plants are so diminutive that they can be easily lost in a rock garden and only make a statement when the frame around them is also small. Using troughs is several aesthetic steps on the way to "natural" beyond growing them in pots in an alpine house. The other reason is horticultural: some plants are happier in troughs, where exposure can be changed or modified relatively easily, where soil mixture and watering are controllable, and where winter protection is more manageable. On the negative side, any care which involves actually moving troughs would have to be avoided by most of the gardeners I know.

So by-passing the discussion of how to arrange plants and how a trough ought to look—taste and aim being very personal matters—I want to mention a few of the plants I have tried to grow in troughs and in their near relation, small raised beds.

We might start with what not to grow. Of course, there is nothing that you couldn't put into a trough if you really wanted to, but it would be perverse to want to grow a tree, unless you were willing to bonsai it, and that would be a different hobby. Nor would you grow border perennials. Actually, even 8"-tall plants look "wrong," unless you stuff the trough full of annuals and trailers as though it were any old planter. But if you want to grow alpine plants with the "right" scale (your judgment), you will want their non-flowering parts to be less than 6" tall and probably less than 2". And when the flower stalk develops, 6" will seem like a very tall plant, unless the trough is really big. Also, we want the planting to last a long time (forever). This is more of an ideal than a practical aim, because mortality of plants in troughs is at least as high as it is on the slopes of the rock garden. What we must not do is plant a robust grower that will spread to fill the trough in one season. However beautiful it looks, you will have a planter and not a trough. The graceful, green waterfall flowing over the edges of the trough is also colonizing the flat spaces of the interior. Don't plan for this kind of disaster. A trough is a terrible thing to waste.

Unsuitable plants are most *Arabis, Aurinia, Alyssum, Iberis* (regretfully), *Aubrieta, Phlox subulata, Silene, Viola, Delphinium, Aquilegia, Campanula, Thymus, Antennaria, Artemisia*. In fact, most plants are not suitable for troughs. You know after one season whether this or that plant deserves a trough. The worst thing you can do is to plant a rare, expensive, but unsuitable plant that hates to be transplanted in a trough. *Arnebia echioides*, for instance, is far too big for most portable troughs and has a root that doesn't like to be disturbed. A dwarf conifer may have to be avoided for the same reason: you may lose it when the inevitable transplant operation is attempted at the end of the year. You could lose the trough, too, in the struggle. I consider plants such as *Ramonda*, auricula primulas, *Lewisia tweedyi, Saxifraga longifolia*, etc., too large for a trough. You may be able to accommodate one specimen plant of this magnitude, but if it is happy, it will overpower a medium-sized trough, and if it is

miserable, it will spoil the effect and die, leaving a large gap that the eye can't overlook.

Another type of plant you may want to avoid is the too happy self-sower. A trough will always look raw and freshly made until there is some self-sowing, and even though a newly planted trough wins a popularity contest at a plant show, it won't impress the *cognoscenti*. A mature trough has volunteer seedlings of good plants along with the inescapable mosses and lichens. But enough of a good thing is all you want, and some species are far too generous. So it may be best to avoid annuals and biennials and plants such as *Chaenorrhinum oreganifolium, Lewisia pygmaea, Erinus alpinus*, and anything else that looks cute colonizing the rock garden too gaily. If I subsequently recommend a self-sower, it will mean it hasn't yet exceeded its quota of offspring in any of my troughs.

Type 1a

Type 1a plants form mounds that grow slowly enough so that even after five years or more you still have a lovable hump about 5" across. Perhaps the most satisfying and satisfactory groups of plants for troughs are *Androsace* and its near relatives, *Douglasia* species and small alpine primulas. I will divide them into types in order to pigeonhole many other species. The first type covers those androsaces that are IDEAL for troughs. *Androsace villosa* var. *arachnoidea* is the epitome of this group, along with its soul-mate, *A. muscoidea*. These beautiful plants are easy-going, too. Growing more slowly is *A. pyrenaica* and its hybrid with *A. carnea*, sometimes called 'Millstream'. These form harder mounds of less fuzzy foliage. You could also try *A. ciliata, A. hausman-nii, A. hedraeantha, A. hirtella,* and *A. obtusifolia* and *A. pubescens. Androsace lactea* is easier than any of them and self-sows generously, so it might belong in Type 1b. The categories are not clear-cut.

Douglasias are American cousins of androsaces. *Douglasia laevigata, D. nivalis, D. montana* are all highly desirable plants for troughs. Some primulas would be at home with androsaces: *Primula minima, P.* x *bileckii,* and *P. villosa* are low enough.

Other plants with this ideal mound or bun growth pattern include many of the drabas. The very best for beauty and amenability is probably something from the complex of species found under the names *Draba rigida, D. bryoides,* and *D. compressa.* I have had various plants with these names, and by now I tend to call them all *D. rigida.* The mounds are hard and tight, and almost indestructible. Expect contented expansion for at least ten years, by which time there will be plenty of seedlings for the new trough you will have to make. (Troughs don't stay "in beauty" for much longer, and you usually have to empty and replant much sooner.) These drabas are Type 1a plants that perform all through the year. If you are one of those eccentric people who doesn't like yellow, just close your eyes in early spring—you can still grow *Draba rigida* with perfect integrity. Other drabas that fit into this mound-making group would include *D. caucasica* (like an even finer *D. rigida*), *D. rosularis* (splendidly hairy and totally impervious to winter wet), *D. paysonii, D. sierrae,* and many of the *aizoides* group (for instance, *D. hispanica, D. hoppeana, D. parnassica, D. aizoides).* But every new draba should be tried.

From genera whose other members might be dismissed as unsuitable are *Arabis bryoides, A. androsacea, Edraianthus pumilio, E. serpyllifolius, E. dinaricus, Jasione amethystina, Eriogonum caespitosum, Degenia velebitica, Gypsophila aretioides,* and the plant everybody wants: *Petrocallis pyrenaica.* Not all the species of *Thlaspi* are worth putting in a trough, but *Thlaspi rotundifolium* and *T. stylosum* are excellent. The best species of *Leontopodium* form mounds, too, even though they don't seem to live very long. Perhaps *L. nivale* is the ultimate in white foliage and elegant form. The western cushion *Phlox, P. pulvinata, P. condensata, P. bryoides,* and *P. hoodii* are all exquisite plants perfect for a trough. Treat *Dianthus* species with caution, but *D. pavonius* would probably behave well enough. One thyme, *Thymus* 'Elfin', and one geranium, *Geranium argenteum,* are not too rampant for a trough. *Helianthemum bryoides* is a tight, tiny shrub that starts off as a bun. *Lesquerella tumulosa* is the best representative of that genus.

Bryoides (mosslike), *tumulosa* (mound-forming), *pulvinata* (cushion-forming), and *condensata* (condensed) are all encouraging specific epithets to look for when you are in doubt about using a plant in a trough. *Nana* (dwarf) also sounds good, but you have to know what the regular size would be.

All the Porphyrion section saxifrages are excellent trough plants. You can also raise the species from this section from seed and get good "troughophiles." Try *S. ferdinandi-coburgi, S. ferdinandi-augusti, S. marginata,* and amongst the easiest hybrids are *S.* x *apiculata, S.* x *elisabethae.* But any hybrid Kabschia is worth putting in a trough. Many saxifrage enthusiasts have troughs containing only saxifrages; since all bloom at roughly the same time, there is a spectacular concentration of color in late winter or early spring.

Type 1b

These are small buns and rosettes that tend to self-sow. Clusters of individual plants rather than notable mounds would be characteristic. *Androsace carnea* and *A. mathildae* are the obvious representatives. Well, you could find a mat of *A. carnea* eventually, but mostly what you get is a lot of small plants dotted around your miniature landscape. These are growing from seed overlooked by the local ants. *Androsace carnea* has some lovely forms with large, pink flowers and some indifferent, leggy whites, especially under the name *A. brigantiaca*. *Androsace mathildae* is always white, with relatively big flowers sitting wide-eyed directly on quarter-sized, hard, deep green buns. Does a single rosette make a bun? As they self-sow, such plants give special continuity to the planting and an escape from the tyranny of the even spacing you are forced to use when you first start the trough.

Other type 1b plants include *Physaria alpina* (not a bun, but it self-sows agreeably), the aizoides drabas, *Gentiana verna* (you have to be good to get this one going), *Primula scotica* (another minor miracle), and *Primula modesta*. By now, I would definitely avoid annual androsaces (*A. lactiflora*, *A. septentrionalis*) which quickly become a nuisance, taking up valuable space and smothering their betters. *Androsace armenum* is biennial and borderline acceptable, being prettier and less bountiful with its seedlings. *Papaver alpinum* in its many sub-

species and forms is also dangerous without constant removal of seedlings. There are many composites that form buns, mats, or rosettes that will self-sow. *Erigeron compositus* is the most reliable, but only allow a really good form to remain (short stems, strong color, tight foliage, and it must have ray flowers). Most *Dianthus* are willing self-sowers and a compact one like *D. freynii* might be tolerated, especially if you are willing to pluck out the larger, more splendid specimens. If you don't, the dianthus will take over.

Type 1c

These are mat-formers that spread by stolons, mostly, but by the time you have a decent mat there may also be some self-sowing going on. *Androsace chamaejasme* is a good example and *A. sempervivoides* an easy one. You may have to remove bits of plant if they encroach on other plants. For this reason, I don't think *A. sarmentosa* is a good trough plant. It will fill the whole space in too short a time. If you plant a trough with other aggressives that can take care of themselves you can have a trough full of color for a couple of seasons. But would you want to use a trough in this way?

Every true mat that roots down as it expands has to be watched in a trough. Some grow so slowly that their tenure in the same trough lasts many years, forms of *Iberis saxatilis*, for instance. The plant may come as *Iberis pygmaea*. Some encrusted saxifrages will take forever to grow into large mats. *Saxifraga paniculata* 'Minutifolia' is one of them, but others grow too large to be in a trough for long. *Erigeron chrysopsidis* var. *brevifolius* and *E. aureus* make low mats of yellow daisies. Townsendias would also make perfect mats, if only they would live a reasonable length of time. Sometimes you get a glimmer of possibility from *T. rothrockii*, but you have to be content with a transient most of the time. *Petrophytum cinerascens* seems to be the easiest *Petrophytum*. The mat is a tangle of fine gray leaves, and the flowers are 2" astilbes. Gentians of the *acaulis* group form good solid mats at varying speeds. Watch that their splendid fat flowers don't steal the space of their neighbors. Many alpine primulas also form mats that look good in a trough. *Primula clarkei, P. minima, P. wulfeniana* are low. Many of the auricula hybrids are too tall and too vigorous. *Primula auricula* itself can form beautiful clumps of rosettes, but in flower it may look top-heavy.

The small western American heucheras form attractive mats with pretty leaves, as does *Telesonix jamesii*. Try *Heuchera grossularifolia* or *H. pulchella*. Several good penstemons form mats or near mats: *Penstemon laricifolius, P. aridus, P. linarioides, P. teucrioides, P. caespitosus*. Some eriogonums form mats without swamping other inmates: *Eriogonum douglasii, E. kennedyi ,* and well-behaved forms of *E. ovalifolium* and *E. flavum*. *Helianthemum canum* var. *balcanum* forms a perfect gray mat and is a mild self-sower. There are many small alyssums such as *Alyssum propinquum*, but in my experience most of the elegant alyssums wither and die after flowering or leave too many offspring.

There is another *Androsace* that needs its own pigeonhole. *Androsace lanuginosa* is a trailer. It sends out long stems that don't root down in any obnoxious way, but in a trough it needs to be planted at the edge and instructed to keep its stems outside the trough. If you want your trough to bloom into late summer, this plant is indispensable. For a similar trailing effect, you might use a small summer gentian such a G. *grossheimii,* or even a fall gentian, *G. sino-ornata*, but their many stems and substantial flowers could wreak havoc unless you allowed them plenty of precious space.

Type 2

These are even better plants than Type 1, meaning more desirable, more beautiful, more rare, more difficult. In an alpine house, they may be easy; in a trough they may only merit the description "possible." The trick would be to regulate soil and weather. One good first move is to plant these prima donnas in a trough you can lift and move. At least you would be able to regulate the amount of sun, and in winter you would be able to haul them into a coldframe for protection against fickle precipitation. Everybody with such a trough should try *Androsace vandellii*, the queen of androsaces. After three or four years you may achieve a perfect grayish mound two or three inches across covered with exquisite white flowers. It will then probably die. But it isn't monocarpic; there will have been a scattering of flowers in the build-up years. And with skill and luck you could keep it much longer. Those that can, do; those that cannot, weep. Close in godliness are *A. alpina*, *A. helvetica*, and *A. brevis*.

Non-androsaces that would fill you with joy but are more likely to burden you with grief are *Physoplexis comosa, Kelseya uniflora*, any *Dionysia, Veronica bombycina, Primula allionii, Aquilegia jonesii, Draba mollissima, D. acaulis, D. polytricha, D. propinqua, Calceolaria darwinii,* and a long list of other southern hemisphere plants. Some of these plants might be quite easy in a climate less rigorous than mine in Massachusetts, or in an alpine house. So try these plants patiently, and only admit defeat when you are convinced they are not worth the cost of a controlled-temperature alpine house. I haven't yet succeeded in raising an *Acantholimon* that was really happy, nor a *Convolvulus* I could be proud of, but if I could, they would go into a trough. *Eritrichium nanum* doesn't really like living outdoors, even for a summer, but *E. howardii* can live in a trough for two or even three years. Another short list of failures includes: *Notothlaspi rosulatum, Paraquilegia grandiflora, Anchusa caespitosa, Campanula piperi, Centaurea achtarovii,* and *Dicentra peregrina.* Difficult gentians for troughs would include *G. froelichii, G. orbicularis* and *G. pyrenaica.* If you grow as many as five of these ultra plants in troughs you can give yourself a ten for superior plantsmanship.

Type 3

These are less good plants than Type 1 in the sense that they are too vigorous for a long-term sojourn in a trough. *Androsace sarmentosa* is the paradigm: An excellent plant in the rock garden, it grows too fast for a trough. You could use it if you were very firm about not allowing it to spread farther than you want. Use cuttings as propagation material. It roots very easily.

A list of similar plants would be endless but would include miniature mossy saxifrages such as 'Peter Pan'. A normal *Saxifraga trifurcata* wouldn't work though. By the time it has reached flowering time the mat billows over its neighbors; hacking it

back then is too late, and the beauty of some large mounds is ruined by indignant scissor-work. Even some encrusted saxifrages misbehave in troughs and don't take kindly to hacking. But if you don't mind growing plants that you will have to discipline, try *Aubrieta pinardii, A. scardica, A. canescens, A. thessala; Alyssum pulvinaris* or many other mat-forming alyssums; *Draba sibirica, Asperula gussonii, Vitaliana primuliflora* and its many subspecies; *Campanula betulifolia, C. raineri, C. cochlearifolia,* and other mats; but not *C. carpatica, C. poscharskyana, C. rotundifolia* or any other rollicking, happy-go-lucky plant that should only be let loose in a large rock garden.

Type 4

There are types of plant with no *Androsace* example: Trees and shrubs. Apart from dwarf conifers, which are almost a cliché in troughs, you could consider daphnes that grow quite slowly in their early years. You would have to find a permanent home in the garden after three or four seasons. *Daphne jasminea, D. petraea, D. retusa,* and *D. arbuscula,* and a dwarf form of *D. cneorum* are all possible. There are excellent shrubby penstemons that can be used to add woody texture: *P. davidsonii* has many forms, and you can find a small-leaved, tight mat. Since you are going to give winter protection to some of your troughs you could try *P. newberryi* and *P. rupicola.* In the open garden these two are liable to get severe die-back. There is a tiny elm, *Ulmus parvifolia* 'Hokkaido', that stays dwarf for a long time. Just be careful when you look for "dwarf" shrubs that the word means small in all its dimensions. You wouldn't want to put in a trough a plant like *Prunus pumila* ssp. *depressa*, which hugs the ground but spreads far and wide quite rapidly. Many mat-forming salixes are suitable for a time but need room to spread. *Salix reticulata* is the safest, the hardest to find, and the hardest to keep. Some junipers would form mats, too. But I think a list of dwarf conifers would be out of place here. There are so many, and it would spoil your fun to single out any of the scores of beautiful possibilities. Other deciduous shrublets would include *Hypericum coris*, *Fumana thymifolia*, *Eriogonum thymoides*. There are a few woody alyssums, for instance *A. davisianum*. But the effect of these little shrubs is more moundlike than tree-like, and none of them takes the place of a daphne.

Type 5

These are plants that blaze away for one season but cannot be relied on to do it twice. They are irresistible for a trough because of reason 1 above (the aesthetic reason) and if you can actually succeed with them, reason 2 (the horticultural reason) comes into play. *Dianthus alpinus*, *Phacelia sericea*, *Iberis candolleana*, *Calceolaria biflora* come to mind. Also, the dwarf lupines from the Rockies: *Lupinus breweri* and *L. lepidus* ssp. *lobbii* rarely stay a second year. Nor does *Mertensia viridis* or *M. alpina*. Even *Polemonium viscosum* is unreliable. You could call them the only annuals worth growing in a trough, except that there are genuine annuals I wouldn't exclude such as *Sedum pilosum*. Townsendias too are always welcome whether they are annual or biennial. *Inula acaulis* is a biennial and *Laurentia minuta* an annual, and both are worth growing.

Type 6

Succulents and cacti may need troughs for themselves. We tend to have immovable prejudices about them, associating them with desert conditions. But many alpines grow in desert conditions, and many cacti are alpine plants. My reasons for segregation would be self protection and possibly aesthetics. Anyway, you can find room for *Coryphantha vivipara* and other *Escobaria* and *Echinocereus*. *Orostachys spinosa* would fit into any planting. Other succulents would include *Talinum okanoganense* (*T. sedoides*), *Lewisia rediviva*, *L. rupicola*, *Spraguea* (*Calyptridium*) *umbellata*, and any other miniature example. *Lewisia cotyledon* is worth a monoculture trough. If well-grown to portly perfection, it would use too much space in a small trough. Sedums, sempervivums, and delospermums are tempting as groundcover, but even the smallest is too vigorous to be allowed near Type 1 plants. Better to try monoculture for them, too.

Well, I could go on inventing types forever, and there are many plants that are useful that don't fit into any of the categories so far. Where shall we place *Astragalus* and *Oxytropis*? We obviously don't want to put *A. gmelii* in a trough, but there would be nowhere else for *A. ceramicus*, which needs all the coaxing you can muster to produce its spectacular pods. Then there are the multiple rosette formers such as *Jurinella moschus*, *Claytonia megarhiza*, *Carduncellus rhaponticoides*, *Crepis pygmaea*, and *Limonium minutum*. Shall we grow *Delphinium luteum*? You can answer questions like the last one by trial and error. If you like it, obviously you find a way to grow it. In time we form our own ideas about what a trough should be used for and ultimately what it should look like. The miniature scene becomes irrelevant. If you insist on a reduced version of Nature, you will think of a trough without rocks and miniature trees to represent the alpine tundra or even a woodland clearing. You can do and think what you like.

Geoffrey Charlesworth gardens in Sandisfield, Massachusetts where he has many troughs and extensive rock gardens.

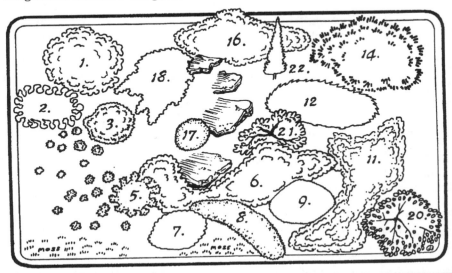

Charlesworth Trough
Years 4-5

—The *Chamaecyparis* was too big, the *Daphne* died. The tufa looks awful, so remove it. Fill the gaps with flat rocks. Several plants are now self-sowing, and a few have become large mounds and mats. The moss is not yet a pest. You have room for a few additions, so why not try some kabschia saxifrages?

1. *Arabis bryoides*
2. *Eriogonum ovalifolium*
3. *Androsace carnea*
5. *Androsace mathildae*
6. *Campanula cochlearifolia*
7. *Draba rosularis*
8. *Saxifraga paniculata* 'Minutifolia'
9. *Draba rigida*
11. *Phlox pulvinata*

12. *Silene acaulis*
14. *Vitaliana primuliflora*
16. *Draba bryoides*
17. *Daphne retusa*
18. *Androsace villosa*
20. *Penstemon davidsonii*
21. *Daphne arbuscula*
22. *Picea* 'Little Gem'

Plants of Pikes Peak, including *Mertensia alpina, Saxifraga flagellaris* in trough, Denver, Colorado

Eight-year-old *Astragalus spatulatus* in trough   photos, Gwen Kelaidis

Penstemon humilis and *Hymenoxys acaulis* in trough,
Kelaidis home garden, Denver

Trough with *Penstemon laricifolius, Phlox hoodii, Haplopappus acaulis*,
Kelaidis home garden, Denver

Plants of Manila, Utah including *Lesquerella alpina, Artemisia frigida*
Kelaidis home garden, Denver

Plants of the Bighorns, including *Aquilegia jonesii, Senecio canus, Carex, Potentilla*
Kelaidis home garden, Denver

Trough in gardens of Drs. Alan and Hilary Hills, Scotland   Dick Bartlett

Edrianthus serpyllifolius 'Major' in trough   Rex Murfitt

Trough Construction

by Michael Slater

A trough is a planter for alpines and other small plants, made of simulated stone. The simulation of an old stone sink or watering trough is a very important part of trough making. A mixture of Portland cement with peat moss and perlite (as a substitute for the sand and gravel of normal concrete) is used. This special mixture is often called hypertufa. Because of its ingredients, hypertufa is much lighter than regular concrete. A trough made of hypertufa can be very strong and durable.

Troughs should be good for growing small plants, long lasting and good looking. Let's face it, making troughs is in fact work. Very few people make troughs for the fun of it, although children can get great pleasure out of the mud pie aspects. Rock gardeners make troughs to grow plants in. If you build a trough, and plants won't grow well in it, or if you don't like the way it looks, you have wasted your time building it. Ideas for designing trough plantings to meet plants' cultural requirements and your aesthetic needs are thoroughly covered elsewhere in this *Bulletin*. This article discusses some recent techniques and refinements of previously described methods for trough construction.

I first learned of the use of extruded polystyrene foam for molds and of fibers for reinforcing hypertufa at the 1990 Eastern Winter Study Weekend. Nicholas Klise shared his methods of using acrylic bonding agents and of metal rings with hardware cloth for large drainage holes. I am grateful for this information, as it has made my trough making much more productive and pleasurable.

DESIGN AND PLANNING

You probably have some idea of the kind of trough you want. First determine size, shape, color and texture you want for the finished trough. Consider the size of the plants you want to grow and the probable weight of the fully planted trough. The proportions of length to width and to height are important. A trough that is deep and narrow looks strange and unnatural. One tall, square trough I made bore an uncanny resemblance to an old milk box sitting on a front porch.

Make a plan for your trough, a detailed drawing or a good mental picture, depending on your experience and how exacting your desire for your trough to look just so.

SIZE

For the purposes of this article small, medium and large troughs are defined as follows:

Small

Less than 12" in the longest dimension and usually less than 8" deep. A small trough can usually be moved by one person without much difficulty.

Medium

12" to 24" in the longest dimension and 6" to 12" deep. When planted, two people will be needed to move it safely.

Large

Greater than 24" in longest dimension and 12" or more deep. My largest trough is 36" long, 18" wide, and 12" tall. Even empty, it requires two people to move it, and after planting two *strong* people are needed to lift it.

Based on my experience and empirical observations, small and medium-size troughs should have walls 1.0" to 1.5" thick when made as described below. Large troughs should have 1.5"-2.0" inch thick walls to be frost-proof and strong enough to handle.

DRAINAGE HOLES

There are several different ways to provide drainage in a trough. Holes may be drilled after the trough has cured by using an electric drill and a 1/2" masonry drill bit to put in as many holes as wanted in the lowest spots in the bottom. Some people like to pre-form the holes by putting dowels in the bottom, packing the hypertufa mix around them and then removing them at the unmolding stage. For those who want large holes, put a metal or plastic ring the same thickness as the bottom of the trough in the center. After the wet hypertufa is in place then put a piece of hardware cloth (metal screen) over the hole to keep the soil in the trough. Put some hypertufa on the hardware cloth where it extends beyond the hole to keep it in place. A metal ring can easily be made from a tuna can or from metal flashing cut with tin snips and edged with duct tape to prevent cut fingers.

No matter what type of drainage hole I put in a trough, at planting time I cover it (them) with material to keep fine soil in and creatures like pill bugs out. I use Reemay (spun, bonded polyester) or fiberglass window screen.

FORMS AND FORM MATERIALS

There are two basic construction techniques for troughs described below. A stable and strong work surface is recommended. The two methods really only differ as described in this section.

FREE-FORM TROUGHS.

Make a pile of sand, the shape and size you want the inside of your trough to be, cover it with plastic and then apply the hypertufa mix until the desired thickness and shape is achieved. Upside-down bowls may be put under the sand to take up space and save on the amount of sand needed for the form. Thus the trough is upside down while you make it. You must lay the plastic on carefully and fold so it lies flat against the mold and the ground around the mold. Everywhere the plastic sticks up there will be a grove or hole in your trough, which may weaken it.

FORMS

The second way to make a trough is to use an upright form and pack the

hypertufa mix inside. This form can be square, rectangular, round, or oval. Extruded Polystyrene foam insulation board makes excellent forms for rectangular troughs; it is both easy to work with and durable. Foam molds are reusable, much better than cardboard boxes, and easier to build than wooden forms. This foam comes in 1" and 2" thicknesses. I use the 1" for small troughs and 2" for medium and large troughs because of its greater rigidity. Ask for Polystyrene foam at places that sell building supplies. I usually get 2' x 8' sheets instead of 4 x 8' because they are easier for me to get on top of my car.

The foam is easily cut with a thin-bladed paring knife. Just pull the knife along at a shallow angle and cut halfway through, then pick up the foam and break it over your knee or on the edge of a table. Cut two pieces of foam to the desired width of your trough, two to the desired length plus the thickness of the foam (these will overlap the shorter two sides). Place your four pieces in the desired position and push long nails into each corner. Then wrap the form with duct tape all the way around the form near the top and the bottom to hold it all securely together. I have recently found that 4" deck screws applied with an electric screwdriver work even better than nails to hold the corners together.

I have given up using an inner form when I make troughs, for several reasons. First, it is difficult to get the hypertufa mix packed in well unless it is mixed up with too much water. Second, I find that I end up with thin weak corners and bulging sides, which is exactly the opposite of what I want for strength.

For oval and round trough molds, check plastic tubs, waste cans, and such at your local discount store for shapes and sizes you like.

Grease is NOT needed to prevent the trough from sticking to the mold.

HYPERTUFA RECIPES

The standard recipe for American hypertufa contains 2 parts Portland cement, 3 parts sieved peat moss, and 3 parts of perlite, all measured by volume. Then enough water is added to make it moist. This basic mix has been very effective for making frost-proof troughs for many NARGS members since it was first published by the Fosters. The proportions are important. Don't put in more cement than the recipe calls for; it won't gain your trough much—if any—strength! Ratios of proven effectiveness are 2: 3: 3 and 1:1:1. With the 2: 3: 3 ratio you will need about 30 pounds of cement, 1 cubic foot of compressed peat moss, 1.5 cubic feet of perlite to make one small to medium trough. Splitting this into at least two batches makes it easier to mix well and fit in a reasonable mixing bin.

Use white Portland cement and cement coloring powders if you want to have a final color that does not contain gray. Or even if you want a gray, you have control over how much. I like my troughs to be brownish or gray-brown. Many different shades of cement coloring powders are available; the browns and black (for making gray) are very suitable for naturalistic, simulated stone troughs. They are not degraded by the strong alkali produced as the cement cures. Look for them at masonry or concrete supply houses. Suppliers who will weigh out and sell you the amount you want in bulk are usually much cheaper than those that have only pre-boxed coloring powder available. You will have to experiment to get the depth of color you want, but start with a cup or so of powder to a batch of hypertufa.

Sieve the peat moss before using it to break up lumps and eliminate sticks from the mix. This makes it easier to mix and mold the hypertufa.

The perlite is used as it comes from the bag. Some people dislike the look perlite gives their troughs and use sand or gravel instead. This is great if you are willing to live with significantly heavier troughs. I find that after a year or two you can't see the perlite any more on the surface of the trough, and even when visible, I think it gives a trough a granitic look.

For safety, use a dust mask when working with dry cement, perlite, and peat moss. Waterproof gloves prevent skin irritation from either wet or dry cement.

ACRYLIC BONDING AGENTS

Modern additions to hypertufa are liquid acrylic bonding agents (for

strength) and synthetic fibers (for reinforcement). Add acrylic bonding agents to the mix when you add the water. Look for an agent labeled permanent or non-rewettable. Available brands include Acryl 60 and Embond. These may make the final trough stronger, but no experimental data exist to prove it. I usually add one or two cups to a batch of hypertufa mix. The acrylic liquid is used in the masonry trade for making mix adhere to other things, as in patching or repairing. For repairs to troughs, mix the appropriate coloring powder with a ready-made mortar mix, and add an acrylic bonder according to directions for maximum adhesion. Fill the crack or break and hold the pieces together for a day or two. Placing the trough in the original mold works very well for this purpose, if it is available.

REINFORCING FIBERS

Fiberglass or plastic fibers replace the chicken wire that was formerly used as a reinforcing material. The fibers—or chicken wire for that matter—are technically referred to as secondary reinforcing materials. As concrete cures, small cracks form. Secondary materials prevent these cracks from growing together to form bigger cracks. Neither material in itself provides much rigidity to the trough, as both are flexible.

Several brands of fiber are available. The only brand I have used is Hi-Tech Fibers. This brand has worked very well when added to the *wet* hypertufa mix as they have a hydrophilic coating. Since the fibers are mainly used by professionals on large jobs, the instructions say things like "use 1.5 lbs.. of fibers per cubic yard of concrete." This works out to 1/10 oz. per gallon of mixed and wetted hypertufa. Since this is a difficult measurement to make, just put in enough so you can

see a significant number of fibers as you mix. Add them slowly while mixing continues, to avoid formation of large "fur balls."

Follow the directions when using other brands. Finding a source for fibers can be difficult. Home building centers may not have them. Look in the Yellow Pages under building or masonry supplies, and when you call just ask for fibers for reinforcing concrete. They will either know right away what you want, or they will give you the telephone equivalent of a blank stare. I get mine at the same supplier who sells the extruded foam. The cost of the fibers is generally modest.

MIXING

Measure the dry ingredients (cement, perlite, peat moss, and coloring powder, if you want it) into your mixing container, and mix them thoroughly. Then start to add the water slowly (mixed with the acrylic bonder, if you wish). The amount of water needed depends on the dryness of the ingredients, especially the peat moss.

Use as little water in the hypertufa as possible. After each addition of water test the mix as follows: Take a handful and squeeze it to try to form a ball that will hold together when you open your hand. When you squeeze the ball, it should be firm and just a little water (a few drops) should come out between your fingers. Instructions on trough making that I used when I made my first troughs called for water to be added until the mix reached the consistency of cottage cheese. Apparently the "wateriness" of cottage cheese varies from dairy to dairy around the country. Many people (including me in my early batches) made the mix too wet.

The amount of water used has a huge effect on the final strength of the trough. Too much water in the mix will cause a weaker final product. Twice as much water will cause the final trough to be half as strong. Work with as dry a hypertufa mix as you can get to do what you want in the way of shape.

As you add water, stir the batch so the material gets uniformly wet. After the mix is partly wetted, I add the High-Tech Fibers a few at a time so they are evenly dispersed. When you get close to the desired consistency, add water ever more slowly, until the mix reaches the firm ball stage described above. The mix should not be runny or pourable. If it is too wet, add some more dry ingredients in the proper proportions.

Many rental centers have small electric cement/mortar mixers available. If you want to make many troughs at one time, renting a mixer renders the job much easier. These mixers will fit into a small station wagon. If you use a cement mixer, you will discover what we have come to call the meatball stage. At the meatball stage, very little more water and mixing is needed. If you reach the slush stage you have put in too much water.

Put down a large plastic sheet on the work surface (sheets of plywood are handy) to contain the mess. Place your form on the plastic sheet. Make your provisions for drainage at this point. Prepare to cover the trough whenever you are not actively working on it.

BUILDING

Take handfuls of hypertufa mix and begin to apply them to the form. Place and pat the hypertufa mix on the inside of the mold, first doing the bottom and then working up the sides. When the mix has the proper amount of water you will have no difficulty in making the walls this way. If you do, your mix is too wet or too dry. Return it to the mixer and adjust. Firmly place the mix, and pat it in so it adheres to the form, making a seamless container of the proper thickness. In rectangular forms, build up the corners a little thicker for strength and to allow whatever material you may remove from the outside to make nice rounded corners at the roughing-up stage. Place one hand on the outside of the mold to support it while you use your other hand to pat and put the hypertufa mix into place.

Once you get the trough walls built to the height and thickness you want, cover the whole form with a plastic sheet to keep it moist. You are done for the first day. Except for cleaning up your mixing container!

For upside down "bowl" forms, apply the mix to the plastic covering the form until is evenly covered with the desired thickness of hypertufa. This may be tested with a nail or wire. Pat and press the mix until it is seamless, except for your drainage provisions. Be certain you make the bottom (what will be the bottom when it is in use) thick enough and flatten it so the trough will sit level. When you are done pull the plastic sheet over the trough to cover it tightly.

CURING

There are two stages to the curing process. The initial stage lasts about 24-48 hours and is followed by unmolding and texturing; for the final, long-term hardening, I recommend four weeks.

UNMOLDING

You have to judge when to unmold your trough. Any concrete produces heat from the chemical reactions that occur as it cures. The hotter concrete is, the faster is cures. Too much heat can be a problem if you are building Hoover Dam, or pouring bridge abut-

ments, or some such large engineering project. On our miniature scale (are we miniature cement contractors just as we are miniature landscapers?), the effect to remember is that a big trough will be ready sooner than a small trough. A foam mold's insulation effect will keep the chemical reaction's heat in and cure a trough in a foam mold ready for unmolding sooner than a bowl-shaped one that is wrapped only in plastic. Generally speaking, upside-down troughs and small, foam-form troughs are ready to rough up after 36-48 hours. Large troughs in foam forms are quite ready in 24 hours.

Gently uncover the trough and feel it. If it feels hard, try to scratch it with your fingernail. If your fingernail scratches it, cover it and wait another 12-24 hours. If your fingernail doesn't scratch, try a screwdriver. If the screwdriver can scratch it, but only with some difficulty, then the trough is ready to be unmolded. Be gentle as you remove the mold from the trough or vise-versa. This is the trickiest part of trough construction, not to unmold it too soon.

"Bowl" shaped troughs can be gently roughed up on the outside before they have hardened enough to pick them up.

If you crack or break a trough, it can be repaired as described under acrylic bonding agents.

FINAL SHAPING AND TEXTURING

When simulating an old stone sink or watering trough, avoid smooth sides, especially the ultra-smoothness that results when the mix lies against plastic sheeting. Avoid also the funny bulges or protrusions that result from too much mix being forced into the mold. A finished trough should not look like it is made of concrete, so all resemblance to concrete blocks must be eradicated during the roughing-up phase while the material is still workable. All troughs exhibit some flaws when they are unmolded. Fortunately, these problems are usually rectifiable.

Roughing-up is glossed over by many people, who say something like "then rough up the surface with a wire brush." I say the trough at this "workable" stage is just the beginning of possibility. You are not quite at the

stage of the sculptor starting with a boulder, but you can do quite a bit of shaping and heavy-duty surface texturing. As a rule of thumb, you should spend at least half as much time roughing up as you spend constructing. Various "implements of destruction" may be used. A hammer and chisel may not be out of place. Try wire brushes, knife-type weeders, the pull style of paint scraper, and stiff putty knives. Flimsy won't do! If the hypertufa is strong enough to handle, it won't be soft enough to work on with weak tools.

After 24 to 48 hours, the hypertufa has hardened enough that you can carefully texture the surface. Shape the corners and edges, and make the wall thickness as uniform as you like. Let testing and experience be your guide for how soon and how much you can rough up the trough. Round all the corners and top edges with a pull type paint scraper or knife weeder. Put horizontal scratches in if you want the trough to look sedimentary. You can gently chisel or chip at the surface with the sharp end of a brick hammer or knife weeder for a rough, carved

look. After the rough carving is done, use a wire brush to remove loose material and to add a little refinement. After you are finished roughing up the surface, there should be fibers sticking out all over.

On bowl-shaped troughs that have been molded upside-down, scrape and shave away the top edge so that it isn't disproportionately wider than the walls below. A real stone trough may look good with a wide top edge, but I haven't seen a big-lipped hypertufa trough that I think looks aesthetically satisfying. Also, make sure to scrape the bottom smooth, so that the finished trough will sit level and not rock.

FINAL CURING

Let your trough cure for a month at room temperature, wrapped in plastic sheeting and kept moist. This will give you the strongest possible trough. BE PATIENT. LET IT CURE THOROUGHLY. The final strength of your trough is dependent on the length of time and the temperature at which you cure your trough. After Portland cement mixes with water, chemical reactions commence that result in gluing together the aggregate of our choice into a final hard product. The chemical hardening of concrete (or hypertufa) is called curing. Curing is not drying! The desired reactions and crystallization will not occur in the absence of water, so the trough must remain moist in order to cure well and reach its maximum strength. Letting your hypertufa trough moist-cure for four weeks instead of one will give you a trough that is about 25% stronger. If you can wait longer, do so. These times apply to room temperature; at cooler temperatures, the reactions are slower and more time is needed.

SINGEING AND AGING

After the trough is cured, let it dry thoroughly. Once the surface is dry, use a soldering or brazing torch to lightly singe off the protruding fibers. Don't hold the torch in one place for more than a moment, or you may boil a water pocket under the surface and explosively crack the surface. Relatively cheap torches are available in home centers for do-it-yourself plumbers.

The trough is now complete, but it must be weathered before use. Back to chemistry for a moment. Portland cement produces calcium hydroxide, also known as free lime, as it cures. Calcium hydroxide is somewhat soluble in water, and leaving it out in the rain for a few months will dissolve away this very alkaline chemical. I expect that acid rain is most effective at this. If the rains don't come often enough for you, an occasional (or frequent) sprinkle with the hose will help. Considering this weathering requirement, it is good to schedule your trough making during the fall and winter, so the troughs can be put out in the weather for three or four months before the temptation to plant

becomes irresistible. Soaking the trough in a solution of potassium permanganate is reported to speed up the aging of a trough, so it can be planted sooner. If you don't remove the calcium hydroxide, it could be very detrimental to your alpine treasures.

Obviously trough making can be an involved, tedious and tiring process, but a beautiful, well-made trough will bring you immense pleasure for many years to come.

Addresses

Hi-Tech Fibers
PO Box 469
Edgefield, SC 29824
1 800 344-1572

Fibermesh Co.
4019 Industry Ave.
Chattanooga, TN 37416
(615) 892-7243

Viola verecunda var. *yakusimana*

Photos by Jane Grushow

Drawing, Rebecca Day-Skowron

Michael and Jan Slater garden on a 1-acre property in southeastern Pennsylvania. They continuously make new planting beds to accommodate a great variety of plants. Mike's current philosophy of life is "I never met a seed I wouldn't sow."

Mike Slater
Oval Trough, Pennsylvania

SIZE: Length 23"   Width 18"   Height 5"

CONSTRUCTION: Made in 1989, free-form, with Hi-Tech fibers.

SOIL MIX: 1 part garden soil: 1 part Calcined Clay Grit: 1 part ProMix

TOP DRESSING: Flattish stream-worn pebbles of mica schist 0.25"-2.5" in diameterLarge rocks are weathered limestone.

1. *Sedum spathulifolium*
2. *Erigeron scopulinus*
3. *Dianthus microlepis*
4. *Cotoneaster* 'Toulon Porter'
5. *Bellium minutum*

6. *Saxifraga paniculata*
7. *Festuca* sp. (2-3", from Bighorns)
8. *Dianthus simulans*
9. *Asperula gussonii*
10. *Lewisia pygmaea*

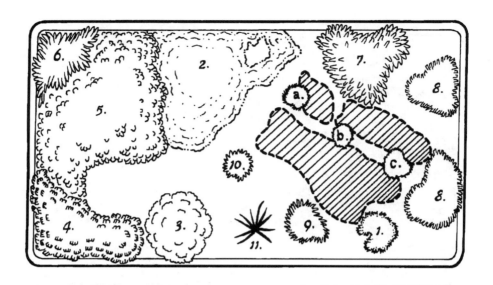

Mike Slater
Rectangular Trough, Pennsylvania

SIZE: Length 36"   Width 18"   Height 12"

EXPOSURE: High shade, morning sun

SOIL MIX: 2 parts Turface, 1 part garden loam, 1 part limestone chips, 1 part ProMix

TOP DRESSING: Limestone chips (approx. 1/16")

1. *Saxifraga* 'Opalescent', kabshia
2. *Asperula pontica*, white form
3. *Draba bryoides* var. *imbricata*
4. *Saxifraga* x *androsace integrifolia* encrusted, Siskiyou Rare Plant Nursery
5. *Saxifraga paniculata*, small form, encrusted
6. *Saxifraga hostii*, encrusted
7. *Saxifraga* 'Foster's Red' encrusted
8. *Saxifraga* x *engleri*, encrusted
9. *Saxifraga* 'Winifred Bevington', encrusted
10. *Saxifraga* 'Lady Beatrix Stanley', encrusted
11. *Mibora minima*, grass
a) *Saxifraga* x *mariae-theresiae*, kabshia
b) *Saxifraga* x *petraschii*, kabschia
c) *Saxifraga* x *salmonica* 'Salmonii', kabschia

Elise Felton
Maine

SIZE: Length 36"   Width 18"   Height 12"

EXPOSURE: Full Sun, due to high spruce trees, eliminates early morning and late afternoon sun. Shade during periods of high heat and humidity. Winter in unheated garage

SOIL MIX: Metromix #360; 1" Terragreen on bottom

TOP DRESSING: limestone pea gravel

1. *Allium geyeri*
2. *Cotoneaster apiculata* 'Tom Thumb', copper-wired to cascade over edge
3. *Arenaria balerica*
4. *Draba bryoides* 'Imbricata'
5. *Antennaria dioica*
6. *Chamaecyparis obtusa* from Joel Spingarn
7. *Draba ericoides*
8. *Dianthus hungaricus*
9. *Thalictrum kiusianum*
10. *Juniperus communis* 'Compressa'

Soils for Troughs

and Other Containers

by Jim Borland

A trough is merely a special name applied to a particular container for growing special plants, and, as such, it differs little or none from a window box, redwood tub, or the pot on the window sill growing Grandma's favorite African violet.

The one dimension shared by all these containers and the one that proves most important in determining how water and air behave in their soils is depth—or more precisely, restricted depth. This same dimension is also shared by soils of fell-fields, shale outcrops, and gardens, but their depths, by comparison, are relatively unrestricted.

In a container, it is the depth of soil and the associated bottom of the container that determine the quantity of both air and water remaining in the soil after the container is watered and allowed to drain. Of the two properties, it is the amount of air and its connections with the surface that determine if the roots in that soil will be adequately supplied with oxygen and have a quick means to rid themselves of toxic levels of carbon dioxide.

When water moves downward through soil in a container, it does so just as it would in a similar soil in the garden, until it meets the bottom of the container. Here it stops, regardless of the material composition of the container.

The meeting of soil and container bottom creates an interface that prevents water from moving across and out through the drainage holes until there is a sufficient weight of water above the bottom to force the water across. When drainage is complete, a picture of the soil in the container will not be one of evenly distributed moisture and air throughout the soil, but one in which each successive horizontal slice of soil from top to bottom will hold increasing amounts of water and decreasing amounts of air. The soil at and close to the bottom of the container will be almost completely saturated with water and nearly devoid of air. The total percentage of water and air held by the soil in the container after drainage is directly proportional to the depth of the soil. The same volume of soil confined to a shallow container will hold more water and less air than that volume of soil confined to a deeper container. In the same way, a rectangular sponge holds more water when laid flat than when stood on end. Neither container width nor total volume of soil in the container has an effect on these characteristics.

This effect of water held at the interface between the bottom of the soil and the container bottom creates what some call a perched water table, and it occurs in any container of any depth and width. Not until the container depth exceeds 2 feet do the air and water characteristics of the soil contained begin to simulate those found in the garden.

It follows, then, that soil in a shallow container will contain less air (oxygen) than it will in the deeper one. It is contradictory, then, that shallow-rooted plants be planted to shallow containers, if, as suspected by many, one of the reasons that these plants are so rooted is that they possess an inordinate need for the higher amounts of oxygen found close to the soil's surface. When such plants are grown in shallow containers with inherently lower capacity to hold air, the grower is constantly attending to watering practices and often heard to complain about "overwatering" problems. It is not excess water that creates continuous difficulties with plants in this situation, but the under-aeration of the soil due to the high water table of the shallow container.

Similarly, the placement of a layer of "drainage" material in the bottom of the container effectively shortens the depth of the container by creating another, higher interface. The container now holds less soil, and water must cross two interfaces before it can exit the drainage holes, rather than one. Instead of improving drainage, pot shards, gravel, and other materials actually *increase* the amount of water in the soil and *decrease* the amount of air held after watering. Single, small pieces of shards or other materials may be used in pots, but only to prevent soil from flowing out through the drainage holes—if that is a problem.

These are only some of the reasons why soils from the garden or from the plant's native site should not be used in containers. Another is the destruction of soil structure that always occurs when these soils are dug and moved to the potting table. Structure, or the physical arrangement of soil particles, is strongly responsible for much of the aeration and water-holding qualities of a native soil. When this is destroyed, and the soil is placed above the perched water table in a container, both air- and water-holding characteristics are severely affected.

These are the major controlling factors associated with the behavior of soil, water, and air in a container. Those who find that watering containers is a chore complicated as much by the vagaries of weather as it is by the danger of overwatering should take special heed of the ingredients used to make the soil mix. But whatever the ingredients, if the final result is a soil mix inherently low in air content after watering, then problems begin at planting and continue as long as the plant is grown in that mix.

Ingredients that can be used to grow plants vary widely, but no successful soil mix can be had by combining fine-textured ingredients with large or coarse-textured ones. An example of this is the mixing of clay, silt, or other finely textured ingredients with gravel, resulting in a mixture that resembles that of a bucket of marbles mixed with a bucket of flour. Neither the water nor the air-holding capacity of the mix is improved. Only the weight has been increased.

Components of the soil mix should be made from particles of uniform size. The more equal they are in size, the less the chance that smaller particles will surround and fill the spaces

Determining Water and Air Capacity of Any Container Soil

1. Select a plastic container as deep as the trough to be planted and tape the drainage hole shut with duct tape.

2. Measure the container's volume by filling it with water from a measuring cup or graduated cylinder, noting how much water it takes to fill the container to the top. This volume of water is equal to Total Pot Volume.

3. Dump the water, dry the container with a towel, and re-fill it to the top with dry potting soil (near-perfect dryness can be attained by heating the soil in a 150°F oven for several hours or overnight.).

4. Measure the amount of water it takes to completely saturate the soil in the container by filling the pot slowly until moisture causes the soil surface to glisten. Allow any components requiring time to absorb water (like peatmoss) to do so, but prevent the evaporation of water in the meantime by placing a piece of plastic wrap over the pot. Add more water if necessary. This volume of water is the Total Pore Space and is the soil volume occupied by air and water combined.

5. Carefully remove the tape covering the drainage holes and allow water to drain into a container. Measure this drained volume of water and label it Air Space.

$$\text{Percent Porosity} = \frac{\text{Total Pore Space}}{\text{Total Pot Volume}}$$

$$\text{Percent Air Space} = \frac{\text{Air Space}}{\text{Total Pot Volume}}$$

$$\text{Water-Holding Capacity} = (\text{Percent Porosity}) - (\text{Percent Airspace})$$

between the larger ones. Mixing particles of varying sizes is precisely the premise behind the preparation of road base (highway underpavement) designed to be dense and impervious to water and air.

"Sharp" sand, a common coarse component of home soil mixes, is always described as the superior sand type, even though particle size and shape, or the qualities of the alternative sand types are never discussed. In fact, "sharp" sand *is not* the superior sand type.

A container of sharp-angled objects, when shaken, will result in many of these objects fitting together, as facets (faces) of the particles meet each other. A container filled with same-sized, equilateral-sided pyramids will eventually fit together perfectly if shaken long enough, leaving no room for water or air. Conversely, a container of even-sized marbles will never fit together, no matter how long it is shaken, leaving plenty of room for air and water. The best sand, then, is marble-shaped or spherica. Sand of this shape is found in some regions as wind-deposited (aeolian) sand. In areas not lucky enough to be near wind deposits, the sand that most closely approximates aeolian sand's shape is usually that discarded by the construction trades because it does *not* fit together.

Space does not permit a full discussion of soil amendments, particle sizes, impurities, chemical properties, etc., but a giant step forward in growing better plants can be taken by knowing at least how to determine the amount of air and water held in any soil confined to any container, including troughs.

With these simple procedures, air and water characteristics for any soil or soil mix in any container can be determined, including troughs. Several other important soil mixing features can be determined as well using this procedure. It can be learned, for example, that air and water capacities are difficult to improve when combining more than two or three soil components. It can also be discovered that the volume of the final mix will often be less that of the sum of the volumes of the individual components. When this happens, the total air space of one of the components has been decreased by the second ingredient fitting into air spaces that existed in the first ingredient.

Some gardeners succeed in growing plants in pots only when their pots are plunged into a sand bed. Plunging effectively lengthens or "deepens" the pot, because contact with the sand allows the water to drain out of the water table at the bottom of the pot into the sand below, thereby increasing the percent air space and decreasing the water-holding capacity of the pot.

Depending upon the depth of the container, most commercial growers strive to attain 20% or more air space in their soils after drainage, and water-holding capacities of 60%, 70%, or 80%—or more. With numbers like these, growers do not worry about drainage (always an ambiguous, ill-defined quality) or give much thought to over-watering, since there is always enough air in their soils to keep roots alive and healthy.

The perfect soil mix does not exist, simply because there are too many physical and chemical variables involved with each of the numerous components commonly used. Several decades ago, commercial growers finally relented and gave up believing that each of their several hundred or thousand species required its own soil mix. Even though each of these growers may use different components, their knowledge of the air and water characteristics of container soils has allowed them to grow everything they produce in one or two soil mixes.

Regardless of the components used in the creation of a soil mix that has optimum air and water-holding qualities, all is for naught if the grower then proceeds to ruin these qualities with planting practices. Excessive mixing grinds individual soil particles to a fine size, thus reducing pore size; pressing the mix firmly into the pot, striking the container sharply on the potting bench after transplanting, or stacking filled containers atop one another all contribute to the physical destruction of the mix's original air and water-holding spaces. All these counteract the effort expended in creating the optimum soil mix.

These and other "secrets" of a good soil mix can be found in any college-level greenhouse or nursery production textbook. Although texts do not discuss troughs or the plants that are typically planted to them, plants are plants, and containers are containers.

Jim Borland has been growing plants for 40 years and has specialized in nursery production and greenhouse production for about 17 years. His interests include western American native plants, rare plants, and horticultural myths and fables.

Planting troughs for Philadelphia Flower Show exhibit,
Philadelphia, Pennsylvania

Finished trough

photos, Jane Grushow

Trough at Royal Horticultural Society Garden, Wisley,
England

Dick Bartlett

Trough in walled courtyard, garden of David Culp, Philadelphia

Jane Grushow

Trough display in Rex Murfitt garden, Victoria, British Columbia   Rex Murfitt

Trough in walled courtyard, garden of David Culp, Philadelphia   Jane Grushow

Monoculture trough of sempervivums in
Royal Horticultural Society's Garden, Wisley

Drilled tufa, Victoria, British Columbia

photos by Dick Bartlett

Angled slate trough at Royal Horticultural
Society's Garden, Wisley

Trough display at Branklyn Garden,
Scotland

Trough of Colorado plants, including *Erigeron pinnatisectus*   Waid Vanderpoel
Vanderpoel garden, Barrington, Illinois

Trough with silver saxifrages
in Murfitt garden, Victoria, British Columbia   Rex Murfitt

Trough with plants of Alps, Vanderpoel garden.   photos, Waid Vanderpoel

Trough with plants of Pyrenees, Vanderpoel garden.
Note that soil in center of trough is lifted vertically by rock placement.

Trough with plants of Alps, Vanderpoel garden, May, 1985

Trough with plants of Alps, Vanderpoel garden, autumn, 1983

Container gardens in San Francisco   Dick Bartlett

Regional trough display, June 1979,   Waid Vanderpoel
Vanderpoel garden, Barrington, Illinois

Troughs
A Few More Comments

*by Waid Vanderpoel*_____

I've been asked to comment on any points missed in the wonderful Spring 1994 issue of the ARGS *Bulletin* on troughs. What can I add to the marvelous assemblage of information, expertise and tips set forth in the six excellent articles which collectively covered troughs—would that we could mulch as completely as this topic was covered. My good spouse read those articles and informed me I'd be writing a very short piece. Nevertheless, I'll give it a try.

Regional troughs
More rock gardeners are utilizing this concept. It is one I have always enjoyed, partly because it provides interesting contrasts of foliage. Regional trough themes allow us to create miniature landscapes aimed at simulating nature—a goal towards which we strive.

How long do troughs hold up?
After fifteen to seventeen years I do observe serious deterioration of the structure of my oldest troughs. However, the modern acrylic bonding agents and fibers mentioned in Michael Slater's articles should extend trough life, possibly dramatically.

Evergreens in troughs
While Anita Kistler would disagree, and her reason is based on solid, successful experience, I do not feel my own experience would support the use of evergreens in troughs over a long period of time. I have two small troughs each containing a handsome little *Picea abies* 'Echiniformis'. However, the roots are so dominant that only one faithful *Erigeron pinnatisectus* survives as a companion in one trough after a dozen years, while nothing else remains in the second trough.

What do you do with a trough now dominated by only a very few faithful old plants?
This is not an easy question, and it is probably best decided by each individual rock gardener. However, most gardeners will enjoy their troughs most if

they own at least containers boasting some relatively young plant communities. Life's greatest expectations come to the young—troughs or people. If a dominating but still interesting plant can be replicated by seed, cuttings, or division and planted elsewhere, the decision to relenquish it in the trough is simplified.

Is there an ideal trough age?

Rock gardeners strive to group plants such that neighbors mature on a complementary scale. Young plants can be introduced into obvious spots, but I find I enjoy troughs where most of the space is occupied by plants of fairly similar maturity. A trough can look mature in three years; in fact, many plants look wonderful after two years. Conversely, some troughs look enchanting a decade or more after the original planting, though by then a number of the first inhabitants are only a memory. Matching trough plants is always challenging, always fascinating.

Troughs in water

Troughs, by variations in size, shape, soil mix, location, and plant material, lend themselves to experimentation. I've had my share of failures. However, I would like to share a winner with you.

I've always enjoyed growing little Aleuritia primroses, particularly *P. farinosa*, *P. frondosa*, and *P. halleri*. The books say they like "damp meadows." On our visits to the Alps, they could usually be discovered, and often by the hundreds, even thousands, near the tiny little brooks and rivulets that drain sunny meadows. However in my garden in the sun, in our intense Midwestern heat, they often wilted and needed near constant attention. I established some primulas in complete shade, where they have thrived to this day, though perhaps they are not as compact as one might like.

I consigned some *P. farinosa* to a small trough and placed it in our fishpool in an inch or inch and a half of water (photo, last issue, p. 120, center left). This was to be the equivalent of a wet, sunny meadow. Since hypertufa is water porous, the soil, even though the surface was 3-4" above the water, wasn't wet—it was soggy! At first the primroses thrived—I kept waiting for them to rot out in the autumn. They looked remarkably healthy for plants about to perish. The little trough wintered in a cold frame and in spring exploded into growth, then into bloom. The tight little plants had considerably shorter stems than those in the shade—but produced a mass of dainty little flowers.

Over the years these little sun lovers have thrived with precious little attention. Every year, there is a surge of bloom, never a sign of wilt no matter how intense the sun, how high the temperature. I've added troughs, tried other species. I later planted several species of *Dodecatheon*, a genus notorious for its tendency to wilt when it is hot and dry. All three species have thrived for five or six years. If you have a pool and like little primroses and shooting stars, give the technique a try.

Species for troughs

After Geoffrey Charlesworth's masterful exposition on species for troughs, there isn't much I can add. Despite the differences in our climates and rainfall, Geoffrey's observations on certain short-lived plants closely parallel my own experience. I'll simply provide observations on plants based on my experience.

Androsace—would be ideal except most small ones succumb in my garden to the combination of summer heat and wet. *Androsace chamaejasme* and *A. villosa* have both persisted as species though with casualties among individual plants. Certainly a premier genus for trial and error.

Aquilegia saximontana—is trough-sized, miniature, pretty, neat, easy, persistent as a species. Has never produced strange gawky hybrids.

Arenaria obtusiloba—seldom mentioned in our literature, but a winner for me. Makes a persistent, attractive, tight mat—even deigns to bloom now and then.

Dianthus—only wee, tight ones which appear at home in a trough.

Draba—lots of potential material, American, European, Asian—but choose the tiniest species.

Erigeron—any small, neat ones are trough material. *Erigeron pinnatisectus*, though larger than many, rates a description such as "particularly nice foliage, faithful, tops in bloom."

Gentiana verna —far from immortal; consider growing more every two years.

Lesquerella arizonica—rather new to me. Tiny, neat, gray foliage, colorful in bloom and easily grown, but expect casualties. Grow a few every year—a small charmer.

Myosotis alpestris, an alpine forget-me-not you can grow. Persistent and trough-sized. Overlooked since it isn't its glamorous cousin.

Petrocallis pyrenaica—a tiny gem from the European mountains. For me, difficult to get past seedling state—BUT the three I own which met this challenge have been with me for a number of years. Give it a try—with special attention at time of first transplanting.

Penstemon—any attractive, smaller, low member of this vast race can be considered good trough material. *Penstemon aridus* has faired very well for 15 years in my troughs. *Penstemon hallii*, *P. eriantherus* (those big, exotic blooms display wonderfully in a trough) and *P. teucrioides* are ones I've particularly enjoyed. Experiment to the hilt.

Primula—in mountain-setting troughs I enjoy species auriculas, *P. auricula*, *P. clusiana*, *P. daonensis*, *P. hirsuta*, *P. marginata* (obtain a good form—quality varies widely) and certain Bernina Pass hybrids, particularly *P.* 'Windrush'. I find *P. villosa* too large, while *P. glaucescens*, *P. minima*, *P. tyrolensis*, and *P. wulfeniana* have all shared one characteristic in my garden—they have a death wish. Hybrid auriculas should be small, compact and floriferous.

Saxifrages—You will try them in your troughs, and you should. They are even more appealing when you can see them up close.

Silene acaulis—One of my top favorites, as much for foliage as its bloom, and can often overcome damage.

Townsendias—ideal for troughs, but given to sudden death. Since they are easily grown, a solution is to have a stream of young plants in our "farm systems."

Waid Vanderpoel has a large, complex garden near Barrington, Illinois. He has been gardening in troughs since 1976.

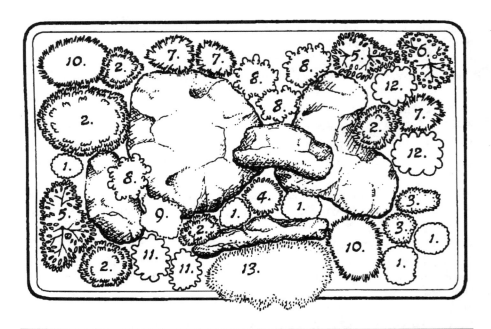

Colorado Rockies
Waid Vanderpoel, Barrington, Illinois

SIZE: Length 36"   Width 24"   Height 8" (all outside
                                                    dimensions)

EXPOSURE: east-southeast, but slightly more sun than Alps trough

SOIL MIX: 2 parts sharp, coarse sand; 1 part gravel, 1 part humus (peat
                                                    and leaf mold)

TOP DRESSING: stones and coarse gravel

1. *Draba*
2. *Erigeron* sp. and *Erigeron pinnatisectus*
3. *Androsace chamaejasme*
4. *Myosotis alpestris*
5. *Penstemon humilis*
6. *Penstemon* (small)
7. *Townsendia* sp.
8. *Aquilegia saximontana*   11. *Hymenoxys acaulis*
9. *Sedum lanceolatum*   12. *Hymenoxys grandiflora*
10. *Silene acaulis*   13. *Arenaria obtusiloba*

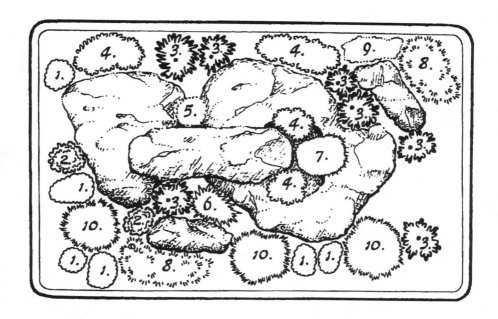

Alps
Waid Vanderpoel, Barrington, Illinois

SIZE: Length 36"   Width 24"   Height 8" (all outside
dimensions)

EXPOSURE: Facing east-southeast

SOIL MIX: 2 parts sharp, coarse sand; 1 part gravel, 1 part humus (peat
and leaf mold)

TOP DRESSING: stones and coarse gravel

—Strive to attain vertical effect with rock placement

1. *Draba*
2. *Petrocallis pyrenaica*
3. *Primula*
4. Encrusted saxifrages, set into holes drilled in rock
5. *Thlaspi rotundifolium*
6. *Gentiana verna*
7. Kabschia saxifrages, set into holes drilled in rock
8. *Vitaliana primuliflora*
9. small cultivars of *Sempervivum*
10. *Silene acaulis*

Hypertufa Rocks

by Wayne Kittredge

Among the memorable events of my rock garden career was the ungrateful upbraiding I received from those to whom I had generously given samples of my latest batch of home-made hypertufa rocks. Winter had turned the soft "rock" into mush, leaving the plants my friends had so lovingly planted sitting atop heaps of ashy mud. Instead of a showy home for a treasured specimen, there was now a mess to clean up. My own rock had suffered the same fate—what to do but apologize?

But my need for tufa was undiminished, so I have continued undaunted to experiment with my hypertufa rock recipe, having as my goal a product that not only looks like real tufa but behaves like real tufa. This year I built a walled garden using my most recent recipe, and shortly after completion visitors claimed to have mistaken the rocks for real tufa.

My first hypertufa rocks—not the ones I gave to friends, but the first batch— used 6 parts peatmoss to one part cement. I built a mound of this in whatever shape the fancy ran to and covered the whole with standard hypertufa mix of 3 parts peat, 3 parts perlite, and 2 parts cement. I cut holes through the layer of standard mix for planting and holes on the bottom for drainage. While the surface was still wet, but after it had set slightly, a culinary fork was used to poke holes shallowly and densely over the entire upper surface to give the rock some semblance of real tufa (photo, p. 224). Over the years, rocks made of that recipe have proven durable. Encrusted saxifrages grow elegantly on them, while *Lysimachia japonica* var. *minutissima* believes it owns every available growing hole. *Dianthus alpinus* submits to life in a planting hole and occasionally spends a few flowers, while *Draba aizoides* flourishes and flowers with its usual abandon, although it does not seed into the fake tufa.

Because the original artificial rocks were performing well, I began reading about the chemical character of cement and other ingredients, hoping to improve on the mix. I got sidetracked on the matter of the cosmetic appearance of the surface of the rocks, trying acrylic paints, waterproof cements, cement pigments, even pottery pigments; none of these were much use, and the kitchen fork method, while very labor intensive, produced the most satisfactory appearance.

I tried more ingredients—perlite for lightness; vermiculite and long-fiber sphagnum for moisture retention; wood chips for their ability to decompose eventually, leaving air gaps as well as humus in the rock; and diatomaceous earth because of its reputation for deterring bugs.

After the mush incident, I overreacted by using waterproof cement as the outer layer over a softer core, hoping for greater strength and better moisture retention. Waterproof cement is, however, pure white and pure ugly, *and* it cracks over winter, although the rocks do not usually actually fall apart. Many plants dislike this very hard and very alkaline white cement, yet others like *Gypsophila nana* and *Dianthus gallicus* have taken to it without complaint, and *Symphyandra wanneri* has sown itself into the cracks and made very neat, healthy rosettes.

The next year I added play sand (a dolomitic limestone available as sand-size grit, used primarily to fill children's sand boxes), an expanded clay

product (designed to absorb liquid floor spills), and grass clippings (or other organic material which would break down fairly quickly, unlike wood chips). When organic matter breaks down, it leaves channels for roots to penetrate, similar to the channels caused in real tufa by water movement during the formation of the rock.

The ratio of ingredients in hypertufa is inexact and is apt to change according to availability or whim. However, if the ingredients are used in the ratio of 6 parts non-cements to one part cement, then the rocks are likely to be durable. Even though the soft core is covered by standard hypertufa, it must be able to retain its own integrity and not go to mush. A recipe I now favor might be: 4 parts Portland cement: 16 parts peat moss: 1 part diatomaceous earth: 1 part play sand: 1 part expanded clay: 1 part vermiculite: 1 part perlite: 1 part long-fiber sphagnum peat: 1 part grass clippings: 1 part a serendipitous ingredient of your own choosing.

Over time, hypertufa weathers and becomes quite handsome, but that can

take years. It's worth spending some effort in applying the surface to have it look natural. The most irregular, lumpy surface looks most like real tufa. The kitchen-fork method previously mentioned has its merits, but I've found a neat and efficient short cut. Apply diatomaceous earth to the very wet to slightly set outer surface. Diatomaceous earth can be shaken or thrown onto the surface by hand (use gloves), resulting in somewhat spotty coverage, or blown on with a rubber ear syringe. Complete coverage of the surface is the goal. Diatomaceous earth gives the surface a grainy appearance instead of the glossy surface of cement. Excess diatomaceous earth may be washed off after the cement has set for a day. Spraying the wet surface with a solution of chelated iron after washing imparts an uneven tan stain. The finished color is a combination of the gray of the cement, the grainy white of the diatomaceous earth, and the tan stain, the whole bearing a remarkable resemblance to real tufa. The kitchen fork method can be used in addition, but I feel it is unnecessary.

Plants already occupying the August 1993 wall built of these hypertufa rocks include: *Acantholimon araxanum* on top of the sunniest, windiest part of the wall, *Aethionema armenum* in the hottest, windiest planting hole, and in crevices: *Campanula andrewsii* v. *hirsuta* in shade, *C. cashmeriana* beneath the *Aethionema armenum*, *C. hakkiarica* in shade, and *C. waldsteiniana* in sun, *Convolvulus cantabricus* on top, *Draba acaulis*, *Draba paysonii* on top and out of the wind. *Hypericum athoum* has posi-

tively filled a vertical crevice with its cute, fuzzy, rounded leaves below the *Acantholimon araxanum*. *Primula marginata* (named clone) has a shady crevice away from the wind and is kept purposely very moist; it is flourishing. *Saxifraga* is already creeping out over the hypertufa surrounding its planting hole, *Thymus* 'Elfin' peeks out at the sun from a deeply overhung crevice. *Teucrium subspinosum* and *Verbascum dumulosum* have escaped their pot prisons into sunny crevices, which I am hoping will provide enough protection for them to survive zone 5 winters. This spring, potted plants of *Campanula zoysii* and *Physoplexis comosa* were planted in the wall. I still have ample room to sow seed and put in plants. The hypertufa rock wall provides an attractive setting for plants that prefer crevices.

Readers might think the alkalinity of the hypertufa could be a liability. However, in my experience, the peat moss neutralizes the alkalinity of the other ingredients adequately. I don't expect to be able to grow the entire range of plants one can grow in real tufa, but I am encouraged by the successes I have had to date.

Wayne Kittredge gardens in North Reading, Massachusetts.

Alpines in Containers
Growing Small Things in Small Places

by Lawrence B. Thomas

I garden in the alpine zone of Manhattan on an eleventh floor terrace—a 13' x 40' strip that some people, considering the price of real estate in midtown New York City, think an extravagance. Others of my gardening friends, who count acres the way I count square feet, think my layout pretty small potatoes. I, on the other hand, have come to appreciate the beauty of small.

While I've grown a gamut of plants, I find myself concentrating on alpines and rock garden plants—mostly because the scale of them appeals to me. I've grown them in large container boxes and tubs with occasional success, but I've found they respond much better to the confined space of a pot, pan, or trough. Like many weeds, alpines seem to thrive when they're forced to lead a hard-scrabble existence. Over-potted, with too much space in which to roam, they are apt to sit and sulk. Give them a little stiff competition, and they'll surprise you with their vigor.

When I first became interested in rock gardening in the mid-1970s, New York City was in the throes of a drought that necessitated severe restrictions just short of outright rationing, an experience that still causes city gardeners to shudder.

At the time, one raffish wag coined the bumper sticker slogan: "Save Water—Shower with a Friend!" While I didn't feel quite that gregarious, I did adapt the sentiment to my own needs by forcing my plants to double up and share their space with at least one friend. By potting them together, I was able to use less water, but I discovered an added bonus—the plants seemed to love it. The competition for root space, for water, for food, seemed tailor-made for alpines, replicating the conditions in which they often grow— tight crevices with little nutriment and water, and a perilous clasp to life itself.

After the water crisis was over, I continued to experiment with this method, growing alpines in smaller pots with leaner, grittier mixes, forcing them to compete for space, for food, for water with companion plants.

We've all seen the way sempervivums languish if overpotted but become a succulent carpet once they're confined to a tight space. I tried a similar treatment on lewisias, planting a clutch of *Lewisia cotyledon* within the confined pockets of a strawberry jar (photo, p. 277). They quickly filled the neck of each opening with their carroty crowns, and within one short season were of a size to put on a splendid display the following spring. Growing lewisias in such cramped quarters discourages rot and rampant growth while keeping the crowns dry. It also allows me to dose them frequently with liquid fertilizer to ensure a good bloom set.

When I visited Linc Foster's garden, Millstream, some years ago and expressed dismay at the cabbage-sized rosettes he was growing upright on a gravel mound, he told me he'd found lewisias to be a clan of greedy, gross feeders, and that it was difficult to overfeed them provided they had the drainage they require. I've followed his advice ever since, giving them a shot of liquid fertilizer every two or three weeks.

I grow many of the lewisia species and treat them similarly, with the exception of catering to their different watering needs at different seasons. I dry off the deciduous ones in the summer and reverse the treatment for the succulent ones, keeping them mostly dry in winter. I begin watering in late February.

One reason often cited for growing alpines in containers is that it allows one to tailor the soil to the specific needs of the plant. Much has been written about the lime-lovers and the "acid heads" of the plant world, and how one must cater to their soil pH needs—particularly those of alpines. Actually, I've found many of the so-called "lime-lovers" to be remarkably adaptable—if not downright indifferent—when it comes to soil preference. This isn't true, of course, for acid-lovers, as most of them are downright picky about their needs and will curl up and die at the first hint of alkaline soil. Accordingly, I pot dwarf rhododendrons, azaleas, primulas, and their kissing kin in the loose, rich, peaty soil they seem to need.

The majority of my plants, however, thrive on my standard lean potting mix, which is 1/4 garden loam, 1/4 peat moss, 1/2 quartz chicken grit, to which I add a tablespoon or so of Osmocote, the amount depending upon the quantity of soil I'm mixing. Occasionally, I alter the mix by adding a very light sprinkle of dolomitic limestone for those alpines that the books say "absolutely demand it." This lean, gritty mixture serves for most of my plants for it allows both quick drainage and an adequate supply of oxygen to the root area. With any heavier soil, many alpines go down very quickly in the close confines of a pot.

Another benefit of container growing is that it brings you into close proximity with your plants. This allows frequent visual checks for disease or pests, and inspection of the pots' drainage holes for slugs, sow bugs, ants and such. Pots are portable, too, and this allows one to shift pots frequently and cater to their sun/shade needs. I window-dress my terrace constantly, putting whatever is in best bloom where it can be seen. My work area serves as a sick bay for any plant that has bloomed out, gone scraggly, or is ailing and showing signs of giving up the ghost.

One obvious virtue of pot culture is that your plants, if you've grown them properly, are ready to show. Many of my in-ground gardening friends dig and pot up plants for competitive showing a short time before the event. No matter how well done, these plants never seem to have settled into their containers and usually can be spotted on the bench. Unfortunately, some of the plants resent the experience and never recover from the trauma.

Two words of warning: Don't over-pot! The tendency of most gardeners is to put plants into pots that simply are too big. Alpines love tight spots, the tighter the better. Some of them are so shallow-rooted that they can be grown in an inch and a half of soil with no problem. I'm not talking just of sempervivums. Many saxifrages—particularly the kabschias—will do remarkably well in a shallow 2" to 3" pot. They tend to spread horizontally more quickly than vertically. My rule of thumb is to pot them up to next width-size only when the bun has reached the edge of the pot. This holds true for drabas as well, unless you want those exhibition-sized monsters that fill a 10" to 12" rose pot and take the blue ribbon year after year.

Campanulas are a different matter. Some adapt readily to pot culture; others simply hate the confines of a pot. The *garganica* group thrives under adversity, growing easily in the tightest situation with the least amount of soil, requiring only that you divide and reset them every two to three years (photo, p. 278). Some of the other crevice-growing forms respond similarly. I've grown the difficult *Campanula zoysii* in a pot that is only 3" wide, 5 1/2" deep. Others, however, require considerable root room, frequently replenished and enriched soil, along with the sharp drainage all of them appreciate. Some of the smaller, running forms, *Campanula cochlearifolia* and *C. lasiocarpa* for instance, resent the confines of a pot or pan and won't stay around very long unless allowed to run about freely. Most are more tractable, however, if given sufficient root room.

An English "Long Tom" pot that is 5" or 6": wide at the mouth and at least 8"to 10" deep suits the ones accustomed to sending roots a foot or two deep into rock crevices or beneath a constantly shifting scree. I grow *Campanula aucheri,* one of the gems of the *tridentata* group, in this manner, repotting every second or third year if the soil seems exhausted. A close ally, the beautiful *C. bithynica,* responds well to similar treatment.

The problem, of course, lies in finding such pots. Readily available to our Scottish, English and Irish friends, "Long Toms" are not produced commercially in this country and are virtually unknown. While some occasionally show up in outrageously pricey garden ornament boutiques, they boast price tags that account for the dust they usually accumulate, untouched on the shelf. Your best bet lies in finding a potter friend and coaxing him/her to throw and high-fire a dozen or so for you. Failing that, you might consider learning to throw them yourself, as I did some years ago when I couldn't obtain the pots I wanted in this country.

I mentioned that I high-fire my pots. Most commercial pots have been low-fired, are quite porous, and are so "soft" or fragile that they will shale and crack during winter months in any area where the ground freezes. High-fired pots are not porous and require careful attention in watering, but usually withstand the alternate freezing and thawing that splinters commercial pots. The trade-off is that they are more brittle and will crack or break easily if knocked over or given a hard lick.

Selecting a container for a plant becomes an esthetic decision, for the pot should not only fit the plant in size but enhance it as well. Be creative in choosing your containers; imaginative, in fact. One of my terrace-gardening friends has a foot-wide, foot-long length of weathered tree trunk standing on end that is covered with sempervivums growing happily in nothing more than the rotted end of the stump. While she grows many sophisticated alpines, this is the show-stopper that grabs every visitor.

Several years ago, both she and I independently of each other, improvised troughs from 2" thick Styrofoam containers in which frozen steaks had been shipped. Since the white surface of the containers seemed a bit intrusive, we spray-painted them. Fortuitously, we found that chemicals in the paint melted the surface of the Styrofoam, giving it a rough-textured look that mimics Hypertufa. She used a blackish-gray; I used a terra-cotta-colored rust preventive.

I've seen terra-cotta drain tile and chimney flue-liners used as containers. They not only make handsome containers but offer good depth for those requiring a deep root run. Even ubiquitous cinder block can be used as a container of sorts. I've seen a splendid terrace herb garden constructed of nothing more than a series of cinder blocks artfully stacked and planted to perfection. Alpines could be similarly displayed.

What to grow in containers? Try any of the alpines or rock plants. A few may resent it and chafe under the conditions I've described, but you'll find many will adapt readily and thrive—some surprisingly so. I'm thinking particularly of one of the rock garden mainstays, *Acer palmatum* 'Dissectum', the beautiful cut-leafed maples that win every heart. Plantsman Barry Yinger makes the point in his lectures that the Japanese devised these beauties solely for pot culture. One rarely finds them planted in-ground in a garden setting in the Orient, though literally hundreds of varieties are grown in pots.

I have six of them growing in pots

that range from a 6"-wide, 10"-deep "Long Tom" to a 14" rose pot. Clustered around a fountain, their lacy foliage is simply enchanting, and they are absolutely spectacular in full fall color.

Species iris lend themselves readily to the shackles of pot culture. I grow a number, among them *Iris setosa, I. graminea, I. prismatica, I. forrestii*. Our native forms, *I. cristata, I. lacustris*, and *I. verna*, like a bit more space in which to run and will do better in a trough than in smaller pots. My favorite, *Iris gracilipes* 'Alba', a perfectly ravishing plant in or out of bloom, is at its best in a larger pot where its fountain of leaves can cascade artfully over the side. Grown side by side with *Hakonechloa macra* 'Aureola,' it is a living sculptural delight of which I never tire.

Dwarf forms of hosta seem tailor-made for container growing. While larger forms take almost yearly division, the smaller forms grow much more slowly and will rest happily in a pot for three or four years. I ring the fountain and larger tubs with their billowing mounds of foliage to give a sculptured look to areas of the terrace. The truly dwarf forms work beautifully in troughs. I have one of my own seedling crosses whose leaves are a mere inch long.

Species *Dianthus* put on a splendid show in the spring, some of them continuing to bloom through the heat of the summer. Over the years I've grown many forms from seed but have come to concentrate almost exclusively on the bun or mound-forming ones. *Dianthus simulans, D. monspessulanus* ssp. *sternbergii, D. haematocalyx, D. callizonus, D. erinaceus, D. anatolicus*, and everybody's favorite, *D. alpinus*, are among them. There are at least a half-dozen more that make good pot plants. Their only drawback for me is that few of the alpine pinks

Monoculture trough of sempervivums in Jane Platt garden. Photo, Gwen Kelaidis

Small free-form trough with *Erigeron pinnatisectus* and *E. simplex*. Photo, Waid Vanderpoel

Aquilegia, Chamaecyparis obtusa 'Nana'. Irene Slater garden. Photo, Jane Grushow

Partly submerged trough with *Primula*. Photo, Waid Vanderpoel

val trough constructed by the late Bob utnam. Photo, Gwen Kelaidis

Free-form trough by Tom Vanderpoel with silver saxifrages, primulas. Photo, Waid Vanderpoel

Trough with slate in garden of Drs. Alan and Hilary Hills,
Scotland

Ann Bartlett

Trough featuring Spanish plants
at Royal Botanic Gardens, Edinburgh, Scotland, 1981

Panayoti Kelaidis

Campanula garganica
several forms in a strawberry jar

Verbascum 'Letitia' (*V. dumulosum* x
V. spinosum)

photos by Larry Thomas

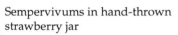

Sempervivums in hand-thrown
strawberry jar

Geranium dalmaticum with
Erodium chamaedryoides 'Rosea'

Lewisia cotyledon and sempervivums in strawberry jars hand-thrown by Larry Thomas

Penstemon davidsonii and *Rhododendron* 'Komo Kulshan'

have much in the way of scent, an exception being *Dianthus tianschanicus*, which is deliciously pungent.

The 8'-long windowsill overlooking my terrace is the year-round home to a group of smaller species *Penstemon* grown in remarkably small pots. I grew them for some time without ever blooming them. Finally, in exasperation, I put them on the windowsill, the hottest, brightest spot on the terrace, and within a remarkably short time, each of them had set flowers. There, year 'round, they bake happily in strong sunlight reflected from the expanse of window behind them. *Penstemon davidsonii* ssp. *menziesii*, several forms of *P. davidsonii*, *P. linarioides* ssp. *coloradoensis*, *P. rupicola*, *P. crandallii*, and *P. pinifolius* are a few that have persisted with never a trace of fertilizer. Despite this seemingly harsh treatment, they put on a spectacular show of bloom early each spring (photo, p. 277).

All rock gardeners are a little soft in the head over that gem of our Western alpines, *Aquilegia jonesii*. Indeed, I'd grow it for its tightly-furled, gray-blue foliage even if it didn't bloom. With a bit of smugness, I can say that without wincing, for I did finally bloom it this year after replanting it against the wall of a newly-made trough that had not had all the lime leached from it. I'm convinced the overdose of lime triggered its bloom, despite the fact that I've babied other plants in the past, growing them in pieces of limestone rubble laboriously toted home from its native habitat in the Wyoming's Big Horns, with nary a bloom to show for the trouble...

Other Westerners that I grow with varying degrees of success are *Smelowskia calycina*, *Physaria alpina*, *Townsendia rothrockii*, *Douglasia montana*, *Phlox condensata*, *Draba oligosperma*, and species of *Talinum* . The lovely prairie phlox, *P. bifida*, and its white-flowered form are one of the spring delights of my terrace, for sheets of it cascade from virtually every corner. Out of its flowering season, however, it can look downright scruffy as the foliage browns off. This makes it an ideal candidate for pot culture since it can be stuck out of the way behind better-looking plants during summer and fall.

Probably the question I am most asked—even by sophisticated gardeners—is: "What do you do with your plants in the winter? Bring them indoors?" The answer is simple: for many of them, I do nothing. A wide range of my alpines stay where they are throughout the growing season—in their pots, naked, so to speak, to the whims of Mother Nature in her Zone 6 mode. Penstemons, dianthus, and phloxes, for instance, come through with no problem. Some alpines, however, demand a bit more care. While they can take almost any amount of cold, they give up the ghost at the slightest bit of winter wetness. Dampness at the crown spells sudden death for these.

In the wild, alpines grow high in the mountains where they are subjected to high winds, intense solar radiation, and wide variations of temperature from daytime to nighttime. During winter months, they are protected from these elements by being blanketed with snow cover that, regardless of its depth, keeps them in a state of dormancy or suspended animation by 1) reducing the light level, 2) keeping them at a constant temperature of around 28°F. (no matter how sub-zero surface temperatures may be), and 3) keeping them absolutely dry until spring melt occurs.

Having lost my fair share of these miffy plants over the years, I devised a system for container-grown alpines that mimics to a degree the conditions they face in the wild during winter. It works for me, and I'll share it with you.

I have two 6' x 2' cedar potting benches that I use as shallow sand plunge display beds during the growing season, then convert to improvised alpine houses at season's end. To the upper worktable shelf, I added foot-long 2" x 4" upright stanchions and connected them with 2" x 1" wood strips, creating an open framework on top of each bench that allows a foot-high space. Late each fall, usually in November, I pack each bench with those potted alpines that require the winter-dry treatment, plunging them into the inch or so of sand, and watering them one last time. Next, I cover the top of the benches with lighting louver (the sort you see in elevators). This effectively reduces the light level, and protects the plants and pots from the harsh sunlight that can thaw the soil and crack the pots. I top this waffle-grid with sheets of Plexiglas, then drape a large sheet of heavy-gauge plastic over the top, stapling it only at the top so that a foot-long overlap hangs loosely down the side of the bench. This allows adequate air circulation but keeps out the moisture.

Though my jerrybuilt alpine house is no thing of beauty, it functions perfectly, which is reason enough for me to overlook its esthetic shortcomings. Midwinter I check the state of things and sometimes succumb and add a quart of so of water to the sand, thinking I am doing my dehydrated, sad-looking plants a favor. I am not, and often live to regret it, for this early watering can stimulate the plants to break dormancy too early and go down as a result. Bone dry is the answer. Steel yourself to this reality, and withhold all water until the plants break into growth on their own, and you'll find yourself admiring your alpines in bloom come springtime.

For my troughs, I use a variation of this treatment. At season-end, I insert four 12" lengths of bamboo upright in the corners of each trough. Over these, I set sheets of Plexiglas that have been cut to allow a 2" overhang. To hold the Plexiglas in place and keep the wind from lofting it around, I heated an icepick, melted holes in each corner of the Plexiglas, and threaded lengths of cord through. I cinch up the cord and and knot it at the top, and make a loop of cord that fits under the edge of the trough at each corner. This holds the Plexiglas rigidly in place, effectively keeping out most winter moisture, while allowing good air circulation in the 4"-6" space underneath each cover. Alpines seem to love it. Even those that I find difficult to winter-over, such as *Campanula raineri*, come through the rigors of winter without a hitch.

Container gardening of the sort I have described is largely a matter of trial and error—of trying and re-trying techniques until you find a method that works. I have a fairly extensive gardening library, but, frankly, little of the gardening literature has been of much help to me. Basically, I have learned by doing, devising and improvising methods that work for me. I hope some of them will work for you as well, or, at the least, encourage you to experiment and find ways that will.

Along the way, I've discovered bits and pieces of disconnected information that have helped me grow alpines and rock plants. Perhaps they will be of help to you. Some specific tips you might consider:

● Forget about crocking your pots and troughs. Use nylon or wire-mesh screening to cover drainage holes.

Your pots will have better capillary action (i.e., soak up water easier and quicker from below), and you'll alleviate the problem of slugs, sow bugs, and ants taking up residence in the drainage hole.

● When potting up mail-order or commercially grown plants, bare-root them first. Do this by dipping the plant gently up and down in water until the roots are clean, then dredge the roots in sharp sand and pot up in your own mix. I do this for two reasons. First, the plant settles in to my soil mix more easily. I've found that if the original soil ball is left intact and planted into a new soil mix, the plant often simply sits there without making new root growth outward and goes downhill quickly. Secondly, this helps alleviate the problem of slugs that has plagued me over the years. People often wonder how slugs manage to get 11 floors up to a mid-Manhattan terrace. The answer is simple—slug eggs arrived in the soil of mail-order plants, hatched, and grew into voracious monsters, necessitating frequent and savage forays on my part. I do it with a vengeance that would do Rambo proud.

While I shy away from chemical means of control because of a cat who thinks he owns my terrace, I did try something different this year— diatomaceous earth, an inert, silica-like substance made from ground-up, fossilized, prehistoric algae, which presumably disembowels the critters. I would say it worked considerably well, for I have seen little evidence of my dreaded foe this summer. On the down side, a gardening friend commented recently that she thought the summer had been remarkably slug-free, that possibly the unseasonable spring might have contributed to it. Whichever, it's a blessing that I accept readily.

● Take a tip from our bonsai friends: practice frequent root-pruning. My method does not involve actual root-pruning but will allow you to put plants that grow too vigorously into a trough or planter-box. Keeping a plant root bound in a pot dwarfs it somewhat. What I sometimes do is to knock the plant out of the pot and tease the rootball apart. Then I knock the bottom out of the pot, insert the plant into it once more, and plant it— pot and all—in a trough, being certain the rim of the pot is submerged. Restricted to the confines of the pot, the roots ultimately will grow out the bottom of the pot, but they spread at that level without rising to the surface. This allows shallow-rooting alpines to grow with less competition from the more vigorous plant. I've used this technique successfully with dwarf conifers whose root systems can quickly take over an entire trough and deplete the soil. Try it—it works.

● Top-dressing your pots with grit will save you a host of problems. It keeps the soil cooler and moister; weeds are easier to pull, and the plant looks better. Quartz chicken grit, if you can get it, is ideal. Turface, an expanded, fired clay product that is used by golf courses to recondition their greens, also works well. I have used it in place of chicken grit as both an aerator in my soil mix and as a top-dressing. It also works well for cuttings in place of vermiculite or perlite.

● Many rock gardeners think of moss as the bane of their garden. I find it can be a valuable and decorative mulch for some alpines. Several of my best plants grow vigorously through a velvety bun of moss, sometimes half an inch thick. I once had *Aquilegia jonesii* growing happily through a thick pad of moss into a limestone wall. Some gentians and encrusted saxifrages also thrive in this company.

To encourage moss to grow on the exterior of a hypertufa trough, puree a 2"-wide pad of moss with 1/2 cup buttermilk, 1/2 cup water, and paint the slurry on the sides of your troughs. Water trough frequently to keep it dampish, and you'll soon have a fine stand of moss. The curator of a beautiful moss garden on Long Island feeds his many varieties of moss monthly with a buttermilk/water cocktail of equal proportions.

● I often direct-sow seed of the same plant under a mature one growing in a pot. Young sprouts seem to like growing in the shadow of their Big Daddy, are easily identifiable, and I don't have to make out a label until I've pricked them out.

● Make your plants share their space. Choose different types of plants for the same pot. Underplant taller growing species or small evergreens with low-growing or mat-forming sorts. Tight, low, gray forms of *Dianthus*, for instance, set off the sharp greens of dwarf conifers beautifully. A mat-former such as *Veronica oltensis* is a perfect understory companion for many plants, though it sometimes can be a bit vigorous. It has taken over one of my troughs, weaving itself into an alpine lawn with a variety of kabschia saxifrages.

If I've piqued your interest in growing these small alpine beauties in smaller spaces, I hope you will plant a few containers yourself and join some of our finest alpine specialists who would love to share their passion with you.

Larry Thomas fell in love at first sight with alpines in pots at Kew Gardens' Alpine House and has remained faithful ever since. He is founder of the Manhattan Chapter of NARGS.

Care of Troughs

by Anita Kistler

My troughs give me so much pleasure! First comes the fun of researching appropriate plants, proper soil mix, correct exposure, and finally, watering needs. Then, planting! Even with all this care, revision is called for. Some plants have romped and almost smothered their wee companions. And plants do die—not many, thankfully.

Location

The first problem is choosing the permanent location of your big troughs. Once a large trough has been planted, it is much too heavy to move. My large troughs with dryland Western American plant material are located in full sun with ample air circulation. Troughs with woodland plants are on benches under a Norway maple where there is filtered light and air movement. Other troughs get morning sun, but noontime protection.

Watering

Weather is the factor that determines watering need. In winter, I enjoy the big troughs from the warmth of my house, and they receive no water from me. The smaller, movable troughs are lined up in the sun in my plastic "alpine house." If they are dry and unfrozen, they get watered. In the growing season, watering is determined by the needs of the plants. Western American drylanders, such as *Lesquerella* and *Physaria*, only get sprinkled. Always remember that troughs are containers, so you are their only source of water during droughts or while they are under cover.

Be sure to locate troughs where they are easily reached by a hose. I use a rose nozzle on the hose, and there is no spotting of foliage or bloom if carefully done.

Fertilizing

Your trough is planted and thriving, and you are enjoying it. The soil mix had all sorts of nutrients when the trough was planted two or more years ago. These nutrients have by now leached out with seasonal rains and waterings. Fertilizer is needed—a low-nitrogen fertilizer. You do not want plants to grow lushly out of character, but only to flourish. For ease of application, I use Osmocote 10-10-10, a slow-release, pelletized fertilizer. I am sure spring would be the best time to distribute it, but seeds, cuttings, and seedlings all need attention then, so September is my time. I apply one tablespoon for deep troughs (27" by 18" by 7" deep), less for a smaller trough. The large Western dryland trough also gets less.

Invasive Plants

Even researching the plant's habit does not guarantee that it will behave as the book states. Do not let a burgeoning plant remain. Remove it, along with as much old soil mix as possible.

Soil Mix

My mix for eastern Pennsylvania is much different than that used in Issaquah, Washington. If your plants thrive, do *not* change your mix. Mine is one part sieved top soil, one part compost (from my maple trees), and one part Gran-I-Grit (starter size) or comparable product. This is a nourishing, fast-draining mix.

Deaths

Even the best growers will admit to plant losses, usually of the rarest plants. Back to the books, or scan your collection for replacements. If nothing is available, consult those wonderful catalogs of rock plant nurseries. And I repeat, remove as much old soil as possible with the dead plant. When you put in a new plant, you can add freshly mixed soil.

Control

Conifers in troughs need judicious pruning. Little pines are candled by pinching the new growth back by three-fourths. Do not use scissors.

Deciduous trees can be clipped to the desired shape. A good example is *Betula nana*. When clipped, it makes a nice, compact unit. Clip azaleas or rhododendrons by July 4, or you will lose next year's blooms. *Chamaecyparis* also needs an occasional pinch to keep in shape.

I have one shallow trough with only an inch and a half of soil mix that has been planted for 15 years with no replacement of plants. The center part is elevated, and a *Picea abies* grows there. It thrives, putting out new shoots less than a quarter-inch a year, so compact at 10". A seedling from the same batch of trees is growing in the rock garden at 30" with loose branching. About a half-teaspoon of Osmocote keeps the four species of *Campanula* that share the trough blooming prolifically and the *Picea* happy.

Lastly, I am upset when a choice plant dies, but I then have an opportunity to choose a new plant. There is always a choice here of more than 250 pots of seedlings. They, too, deserve a home in one of my 35 troughs.

Anita Kistler is an expert gardener, grower, and shower of plants. She gardens in West Chester, Pennsylvania.

Tips on Troughs

by Rex Murfitt

Soil Mixture

Over the years I have modified my soil mixture from the lean, mean alpine mix so often recommended to one with a little more body in it. This is achieved by increasing the amount of organic matter by 50% by the addition of leaf mold to peatmoss and by reducing the amount of topsoil.

I delete sand in favor of gravel, often referred to as grit. I prefer grit screened from my coarse sand mixed equally with purchased poultry grit. Such a blend provides a range of particle sizes that are important in the air and water relationships within the soil. This coupled with the extra organic matter increases the moisture holding capacity of the soil.

Top-dressing

Again, I prefer screenings from coarse sand. The exact size of the grit is not as critical as removing all the fine particles by screening over wire mesh similar to window screening. It is easy to pick out large or otherwise unsuitable pieces at the same time. Apply the mulch as heavily as possible on the surface of the trough, and let it remain loose, so there are no stable areas where liverwort and moss can get a foothold. Top-dressing does not prevent weed seeds from germinating, but, on the other hand, it does encourage self-sowing of choice alpines on the surface of the trough. It is advisable to avoid uniform-sized or colorful dressings, such as those lovely golden stucco stones or glaring white marble. Stay with the mid-gray colors similar to the aggregates of your local concrete.

Stone for Troughs

I re-use, whenever required, several pieces of very light pumice collected years ago somewhere in the West by Boyd Kline. The rocks are all roughly the size of two loosely clenched fists and a lovely, ochre-yellow color. All are extremely porous, which the roots love. Furthermore, the color blends well with the gray shades of the concrete. Tufa is an ideal material and somewhat easier to obtain. Be sure that you get the soft, porous variety rather than the hard, glassy kind. Recently, I landscaped a trough using a stratified, slate-like rock of local origin, placing it on edge, as in the pictures we see from Czechoslovakia. I admit I based my design on a beautiful trough I saw at Wisley. Interesting effects can be created by using stones of varying thickness and depth.

Landscaping a Trough

Since the rocks are the backbone of the landscape, it is vital that they be exploited to the utmost, particularly if your supply is limited, and the rocks are not as big as you would prefer. Group them together rather than scattering them over the surface, so that you make a statement rather than risk a flat, uninteresting scene.

Select three rocks, one large and two smaller, and play with them until they form a pleasing group. Arrange them in a generally triangular pattern with the larger one set a few inches in from one corner of the trough. Leave about an inch of planting space between the rocks.

Flat pieces of stone can be made attractive by layering them together as bread in a sandwich. Soil and rock fragments plus plants are packed in the space where the filling of the sandwich would be, creating ideal conditions for drabas and saxifrages. Then, standing the entire stack on edge, bury the bottom third or half in the soil of the trough.

Needless to say, large pieces of nicely shaped tufa are the easiest with which to work; often one piece will be enough for a whole trough. If you feel that you have limited your planting space because there is so much rock in the trough, drill into the tufa on the top or on the sides. Such holes provide ideal homes for many a choice plant.

Trees and Shrubs

Deciduous and evergreen trees and shrubs are major elements in your design and must be considered at the same time as the rocks. Do not be afraid to use a fairly large specimen,

preferably pot-grown. Plant such woody plants as close to the side of the container as possible and never in the very center—remember art class! Besides looking better, this also permits the branches to hang over the side of the container where they won't smother precious planting space. Put trees as close to the major rockwork as the rootball will allow. If all is correct, rocks and miniature shrubs will set each other off nicely; if not, you will quickly recognize that the scale is off and change something

Tree roots soon grow and fill the trough and compete with other plants for nutrients. While most alpine plants don't seem bothered by this, it is very difficult to get sufficient water into the soil during dry weather. Guard against this by watering in several applications rather than one large dose.

Placing the Plants

When you are satisfied with the rocks, trees, and shrubs, it is time to consider the remaining plants. First, in what location will the trough be placed? Will it be sunny, shady, windy? Select plants that will be compatible with the growing conditions. If you are lucky enough to have choices, it is fun to design special purpose gardens. Think of one planted with *Gaultheria, Soldanella*, and dwarf mossy saxifrages. I am fortunate to have a trough filled solely with *Gentiana sino-ornata*. For special plants, special soils can be created, and I have even made small lath shades for some.

Do not feel that you must use only rare and difficult varieties in your troughs. One of my favorite containers is planted with lots of tufa, a nicely shaped pot-grown grafted pine (name not known) and sempervivums. True, the sempervivums were selected for bright color, small stature, and degree of hairiness. It gives me pleasure to point out to frustrated visitors that it is easy to succeed with such a planting scheme.

Take care not to crowd the plants by planting too many. It is a temptation to plant for immediate effect, but later you will be faced with having to remove plants, and some choice plants do not like being moved. If you want to fill the space right now, it is wise to plant such things as small sempervivums and sedums or even encrusted saxifrages, which do not mind disturbance.

Plant tiny and cushion-forming alpines in the higher crevices, clump-forming types at the base of the miniature cliffs, and the creeping kinds on the lower elevations where they cannot overrun smaller plants but are free to creep to the sides, hopefully to overhang the edge.

Mistakes are easily made. Do not plant the carpeting raoulias wherever you live, for even if they do not last through the winter, they will take over a trough during the growing season. The same can be said for cute little *Oxalis*, filmy *Parahebe*, *Paronychia*, even sweet little *Campanula cochlearifolia*. *Dryas octopetala*, including the dwarf form, should be used with extreme caution. Phloxes make good fillers, but even the *P. douglasii* forms will get too big eventually. Use them until they do, and then move them to the garden.

Rex Murfitt worked as a nurseryman at W.E.Th. Ingwersen's Birch Farm Alpine Plant Nursery. His interest in troughs was rekindled while manager at Stonecrop Nurseries in Cold Spring, New York. He now has 15 troughs in his garden in Victoria, British Columbia.

Rebecca Day-Skowron

Townsendia exscapa

Wallace Wood
San Francisco

SIZE: Length 14"   Width 14"   Height 8" outside, 7" inside

EXPOSURE: Full sun

SOIL MIX: Peat, sand, gravel in equal parts

TOP DRESSING: Cracked granite 1/8" to 1/4"

—Used for display and to promote sales of alpine-type plants at Strybing Arboretum plant sales. Constructed 1985. Plant 7 is over plant 8, making a long spring-to-summer blooming units. See ARGS *Bulletin Vol. 48(2)* for drawing of wooden container.

1. *Scleranthus biflorus*
2. *Erodium chamaedryoides* 'Roseum'
3. *Azorella trifurcata* (*Bolax*)
4. *Jasminum parkeri*
5. *Androsace sarmentosa* var. 'Chumbyi'
6. *Hypericum empetrifolium* 'Prostatum'
7. *Armeria juniperifolia* 'Bevan's Variety'
8. *Rhodohypoxis baurii* 'Tetra Rose'
9. *Chamaecyparis pisifera* 'Plumosa Nana Aurea'
10. *Pieris japonica* 'Pygmaea'

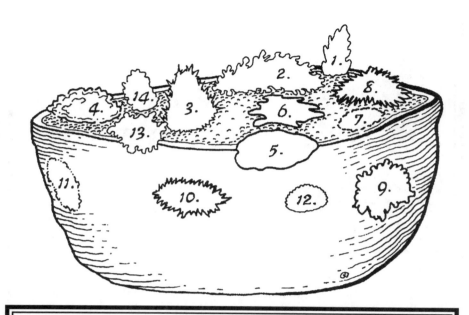

Wayne Kittredge
Massachussetts

SIZE: Length 23"   Width 19"   Height 12"

EXPOSURE: Full sun

SOIL MIX: Leaf mold, manure, clay sod (rotted), vermiculite, perlite, grit

TOP DRESSING: 3" deep coarse grit and gravel

COMMENTS: Crevices in the sides of the trough extend through to interior soil, so that the lip of the trough provides an overhang that protects from moisture on the foliage.

1. *Gentiana* sp., 12" tall, June flowers
2. *Potentilla nitida*
3. *Carlina acanthifolia*
4. *Viola variegata*
5. *Ajania xylorrhiza*
6. *Verbascum acaule*
7. *Paronychia chionea*
8. *Dianthus* sp.
9. *Arabis bryoides*
10. *Dianthus* sp.
11. *Arenaria* sp., chartreuse foliage
12. *Draba polytricha*
13. *Potentilla nevadensis*
14. *Penstemon angustifolius*

NORTH AMERICAN ROCK GARDEN SOCIETY

The North American Rock Garden Society is for gardening enthusiasts interested in alpine, saxatile, and low-growing perennials. It encourages the study and cultivation of wildflowers that grow well among rocks. NARGS provides extensive opportunities for both beginners and experts to expand their knowledge of plant cultivation and propagation, and of construction, maintenance, and design of special interest gardens. NARGS has more than 4,000 members in the US, Canada, and 30 other nations and offers many valuable services .

QUARTERLY BULLETIN
Rock Gardening Quarterly is published every three months. Articles are contributed by members around the world on a wide range of subjects involving alpines and other wildflowers: methods of propagation from seeds and cuttings; special sites in the garden for particular plants; origins of specific plants; detailed accounts of plants in the wild; hints on cultivation, etc. Color photos and pen-and-ink drawings add visual information. Included also are advertisements offering a variety of services valuable to gardeners.

SEED EXCHANGE
Each year NARGS prints a list of seeds donated by its members around the world. Recent lists have had over 5,000 entries, seeds mostly unavailable from commercial sources.

MEETINGS & LECTURES
Local Chapters meet throughout the year for lectures, exchange of plants and seeds, shows, and garden visits. There is an Annual National Meeting The site changes from year to year. There are also two Winter Study Weekends

BOOKSTORE, SLIDE LIBRARY, LIBRARY LOAN SERVICE
NARGS maintains a mail-order bookstore that offers horticultural books and other pertinent material to members at a discount. Individuals and horticultural groups many rent slide shows and videotapes. There are sets dealing with many aspects of alpines and wildflowers, in the wild and in cultivation. Each series is accompanied by a detailed information sheet. By special arrangement with Pennsylvania Horticultural Society, North American members may borrow books by mail for a small fee.

TO JOIN, WRITE: J. Mommens, Exec. Secretary, PO Box 67, Millwood, NY 10546 USA. Membership $US25, £17 Sterling, $32 Canadian per year; Patron $75 per year; Life Member (40-59 years of age) $500; Life Member (60 years of age or older) $450

INDEX